D0876773

CRIMINAL LAW
FOR
THE LAYMAN

Inbau Law Enforcement Series

CRIMINAL LAW
FOR
THE LAYMAN

A Guide for Citizen and Student

FRED E. INBAU
Professor of Law, Northwestern University

MARVIN E. ASPEN
Head of Appeals and Review Division,
City of Chicago Law Department

CHILTON BOOK COMPANY
RADNOR, PENNSYLVANIA

343

Inbau

Copyright © 1970 by Fred E. Inbau and Marvin E. Aspen

First Edition

All rights reserved

Published in Radnor, Pa., by Chilton Book Company
and simultaneously in Ontario, Canada,
by Thomas Nelson & Sons, Ltd.

ISBN   0-8019-5415-0   *Cloth Edition*
ISBN   0-8019-5598-X   *Paper Edition*

Library of Congress Catalog Card Number 72-128868

Manufactured in the United States of America

Second Printing, September 1973

To MARIE D. CHRISTIANSEN
from F.E.I.
To GEORGE and HELEN ASPEN
from M.E.A.

Preface

Although the average citizen has always been curious about criminal law and its administration, his principal source of information has been generally inadequate, and frequently distorted—the offerings of the movies, television, novels and other media. In the past, the consequences of this limitation were not disturbing to, or even recognized by, the ordinary viewer or reader. The general public welfare and safety were, themselves, little affected. But events of the past decade or so have made it imperative that this limitation be lifted, and that accurate information be made available.

Today's citizen is very much concerned about crime and the law governing criminal conduct. He wants to know more about the legal controls against crime and about legal safeguards for those accused of crime. His interest is based on more than civic concern alone—the not unreasonable fear that he, or members of his family, or his close friends, may someday become involved in the processes of the criminal law, as witnesses, suspects, or even victims.

Another basis for citizen interest in criminal law is the possibility of a call for jury service in a criminal case. In that event, a reasonable acquaintance with the fundamentals of criminal law and its administration will render that civic duty the more interesting, and the more effective.

This book was prepared to satisfy the need of the layman and the student for easily understood facts about criminal law and its application on all levels—on the street, in the police station, in the trial courts, in the appellate courts. We trust and believe it measures up to that objective.

Fred E. Inbau
Marvin E. Aspen

Contents

Part II
LEGAL PROCESSES, FROM ARREST TO APPEAL

Part III
CRIMINAL LAW ADMINISTRATION

xvi

Contents

Part I CRIMES

Chapter 1

Crimes Against the Person

HOMICIDE

Homicide is the killing of one person by another, but not all homicides are criminal. For instance, a person who kills another in self-defense has committed no crime; it is a "justifiable" homicide. The same is true of a police officer who kills a person to prevent a felony such as robbery or burglary, and the killing is a necessary preventive measure. It is also justifiable homicide when an officer kills a dangerous felon in order to prevent his escape. Some killings are "excusable" homicides, as when a person accidentally, and without gross negligence, causes death. A killing amounts to a "criminal" homicide when it is committed without lawful justification or excuse. Depending on certain circumstances, it may be either "murder" or "manslaughter."

In colonial America, and before that in England, murder and manslaughter were prescribed by court decisions, which came to be known as the "common law." Since then, murder and manslaughter have been redefined in most jurisdictions by the legislatures, either in the form of separate statutes or as provisions of a criminal code.

3

Murder

According to common law, murder was a killing with "malice," and the requirement of malice is still found in some statutes and codes. The California Penal Code has retained it and provides, as did common law, that

> ". . . malice may be express or implied. It is express when there is manifested a deliberate intention to take away the life of a fellow creature. It is implied, when no considerable provocation appears, or when the circumstances attending the killing show an abandoned and malignant heart."

A clear illustration of express malice is the case in which one person intentionally pushes another off a mountainside. An example of implied malice is the case in which a person fires a rifle at a moving passenger train, just to scare the persons aboard or to display his skill at firing a bullet between the cars without hitting anyone. The danger inherent in such conduct would be evidence of malice in any killing that may be reasonably attributed to such conduct. It would indicate, to a California court or jury, "an abandoned and malignant heart."

Felony-Murder

Another example of malice is a killing during the course of a felony, such as robbery. Even though a robber's gun fires accidentally, killing the robbery victim, a bystander or a police officer, his conduct in committing a felony satisfies the legal requirement of malice, so that the killing becomes punishable as murder. A similar line of reasoning has resulted in holding co-felons guilty of murder when, in the course of an exchange of shots between robbers and police, a police officer is accidentally killed by another officer.

Malice may be attributed to a robber whose partner intentionally kills someone during commission of the robbery or during attempted escape. Malice by all participants is implied in the danger inherent in the robbery itself; each robber is considered to act as an agent for the others in accomplishing their objective, including the attempt to escape.

The issue of felony-murder stems primarily from the prosecution's interest in seeking the death penalty for such killings. In some of the states that have abolished capital punishment (Wisconsin, for example), the legislatures, in order to punish robbers more severely whenever a killing results, have provided that the punishment for such offenses be fifteen years greater than that provided for robberies.

Degrees of Murder

Some states have specified varying penalties for murder, depending upon the circumstances of the killing. A "willful, deliberate and premeditated" killing, such as a poisoning or a killing during the commission of a forcible felony, may be labeled first degree murder and punishable by death or long imprisonment. Other forms of murder may be of second degree and punishable by a lesser penalty. According to common law there were no degrees of murder; any unlawful killing was either murder or manslaughter.

Manslaughter

Manslaughter was defined by common law as an unlawful killing without malice, and was classified as either "voluntary" or "involuntary." Manslaughter, in contrast to murder, is usually punishable by a prison term of from one year to ten or fourteen years.

Voluntary Manslaughter

An intentional killing after "great provocation" and "in the heat of passion" constitutes the crime of voluntary manslaughter. A classic example is the killing of one member of a married couple by the other member who unexpectedly finds his or her spouse in an act of sexual intercourse, or in a situation that indicates impending or concluded adulterous conduct. A killing of the paramour or of the spouse, or both, in such a circumstance would fall within the category of manslaughter because the provocation was great and the killer was in the heat of passion.

Such a killing is treated less harshly than murder because the law holds a sympathetic appreciation of the instinctive reaction to kill whenever a husband or a wife is confronted with such a situation. Nevertheless, the view generally prevails that such conduct should be discouraged by criminal sanction, but one with a penalty considerably less than that for murder.

The conviction rate in such killings is quite low, primarily because of the occasional willingness of juries to accept the frequently concocted explanation that the killing occurred in self-defense, when the paramour attacked the spouse, who killed his attacker only in order to keep from being killed himself. Acquittal in such cases is sometimes described in the press to have resulted by reason of "the unwritten law."

A few states (Texas, New Mexico and Utah) have tried to simplify the complications of paramour killings by providing legal pardon when the paramour is caught in the act. But in those states the privilege does not extend to the killing of the participating spouse.

In applying the test of whether or not an intentional killing was committed after great provocation and in the heat of passion, a lawyer asks the jury, or the judge in non-jury cases, to consider whether or not the accused reacted as a "reasonable" man. Technically speaking, the particular sensitivity or temper of the killer is not taken into consideration. Instead, an effort is made to determine how a "reasonable" man might have acted under similar circumstances. An apt illustration is a famous English case in which a sexually impotent man felt insulted by the remarks of a prostitute with whom he had tried in vain to have sexual intercourse, and proceeded to kill her. He contended that his sensitivity about his condition should be taken into account in determining whether or not there was serious provocation for his reaction, but the court held that his conduct was to be judged by the standard of an ordinary, normal "reasonable" man.

Involuntary Manslaughter

In general, involuntary manslaughter may be described as an unintentional killing resulting from gross negligence, or as a result of dangerous and unlawful conduct. A person may be guilty of manslaughter if he throws a heavy object from an upper floor of a building into an alley frequently used by pedestrians and the object kills someone. Similarly, a motorist who is traveling at an excessive speed may be guilty of manslaughter if he kills a child at a school crossing.

A number of states have created a related crime known as "reckless homicide" or "negligent homicide," which applies to killings by motorists who were driving in a reckless or grossly negligent manner. Such special homicide legislation was enacted because of the difficulty of convicting motorists for manslaughter, which not only sounded like a horrible crime but also carried a minimum penalty of one year in the penitentiary. It was thought advisable to categorize such conduct with the less revolting label of reckless or negligent homicide and also to permit the imposition of lesser penalties than those prescribed for manslaughter. For the sake of justice, a reasonable number of convictions carrying relatively light penalties is more desirable than few convictions carrying heavy penalties. The permissible range of penalties in reckless or negligent homicide statutes is generally a fine of up to $1,000, or incarceration, other than in a penitentiary, for a period of up to one year, or imprisonment in a penitentiary for up to five years. (When the traffic victim of such conduct does not die, another statutory offense may be invoked: "reckless conduct.")

The flexibility of penalties in traffic death cases has had the effect of encouraging pleas of guilty from offenders, and it has resulted in convictions that might not have been secured if a judge or jury had no choice other than a penitentiary sentence or acquittal.

Federal Homicide Law

There is no general federal homicide law. There can be none, in fact, because there is no constitutional authority for Congress to legislate the subject except in cases involving killings within a federal territory, in federal buildings or on federal property, or killings of federal officials, officers or other personnel.

Examples

1. Without justification or excuse, Jack shoots and kills Frank in a Post Office. Jack has committed a federal offense of criminal homicide.

2. Hank, a fugitive bank robber about to be apprehended by an FBI agent, shoots and kills the agent. Hank is guilty of a federal crime of murder.

Modern Murder-Manslaughter Legislation

In most states, the statutes covering murder and manslaughter are patterned after common law. The law is slowly becoming more modern, however, as the 1961 Illinois Criminal Code demonstrates. In defining murder, for instance, it avoids such language as "malice" and "abandoned and malignant heart," and uses more precise terminology.

According to the Illinois Code, a person who kills another individual "without lawful excuse" commits murder if he "intended" to kill him or to do great bodily harm; if, without intending to kill, it clearly appears that he "must have known" that his conduct would probably cause death; or if death resulted from "the commission of a very serious crime" like robbery, burglary, or rape.

Capital Punishment

For many years the controversy has continued about how effectively capital punishment serves its intended purpose, that of deterring murder. However, because of the rapid decline in executions in recent years, the question of capital punishment has become rather academic. While there were 199 executions in 1935, there was only one in the entire United States in 1966, two in 1967, and none in 1968 or 1969. Yet, in each of those four years, over 500 persons were under sentence of death.

In addition, a legal concept was recently enunciated by the Supreme Court of the United States that will make jury imposition of the death penalty much more difficult to obtain. The court held that prospective jurors in capital cases could not be rejected solely because they objected to the death penalty. To do so, said the Court, constitutes a deprivation of due process because the defendant would not then be accorded a trial by a "fair

and impartial jury." Exclusion because of such beliefs
alone is permissible only when the prospective juror states
that he would not consider setting aside his beliefs in the
particular case for which he was called for jury duty.

KIDNAPPING AND UNLAWFUL RESTRAINT

A kidnapping occurs when a person is unlawfully seized
and secretly confined against his will.

> *Example*
> Mr. and Mrs. Kay seize Suzie, a six-year-old.
> They take her in their car to a cottage in the
> country and make contact with Suzie's parents
> to demand a ransom payment. The Kays are
> guilty of the crime of kidnapping.

Kidnapping also occurs when an individual, by deceit,
by enticement, or by force or threat of force, induces
another person to go from one place to another with the
intent of secretly confining that person against his will.

> *Example*
> Joe and Bill meet Joyce at the neighborhood
> bar. When the bar closes, they promise to drive
> Joyce home. Instead, they take her to Joe's
> home, where they advise her she will be kept
> prisoner until she obliges them with her sexual
> favors. At this point, Joe and Bill have com-
> mitted the offense of kidnapping.

In many jurisdictions, the confinement of a child under
the age of thirteen is considered, by law, to be against the
will of the child regardless of any purported consent on
the child's part. In many states, the penalty for kidnapping a child is greater than that for kidnapping an
adult. If a kidnapping is committed while the perpetrator

is masked or hooded, or if the victim is seriously harmed physically, a greater penalty is provided. When a kidnapping is for the purpose of obtaining a ransom or any other valuable concession, some states impose the death penalty.

Kidnapping becomes a federal crime, as well as a state crime, whenever any elements of the offense occur in more than one state. The constitutional basis for the federal kidnapping law in such situations is the constitutional power of Congress to regulate "interstate commerce."

Example

Joe and Doug kidnap a six-year-old in State A and take him to State B, where they hold him pending the delivery of a ransom payment from his father. The federal kidnapping law has been violated because of the interstate scope of the crime. (Joe and Doug can also be prosecuted in State A and in State B for violations of the kidnapping laws of those states.)

The federal kidnapping statute was enacted in 1932, shortly after the kidnapping and death of the son of the famous aviator, Charles A. Lindbergh. In 1934, the statute was amended to provide that after the lapse of seven days a presumption arose that the kidnapped person had been taken from one state to another. The purpose of the amendment was to permit the FBI to enter the investigation, which otherwise would have remained exclusively one for the state to conduct until subsequent events established a crossing of state lines.

In 1956, following an inept handling of the investigation of a kidnapping by local authorities, and a newspaper leak that resulted in the death of the kidnapped infant, the presumptive period of interstate transportation was

reduced to twenty-four hours. Consequently, the FBI may
now officially enter the investigation of a kidnapping
twenty-four hours after its occurrence. However, as soon
as subsequent events establish that there has been no
transportation of the kidnapped person outside the state,
the FBI authority ceases; the case then becomes one
within the exclusive jurisdiction of state and local police
agencies.

An offense of unlawful restraint occurs when a person
is detained without legal authority, even though there
may have been no intent to confine the victim secretly.
The penalty for unlawful restraint is less severe than that
for kidnapping.

> *Example*
> Bessie Busybody, a housewife, observes Tillie
> Teen at the phonograph counter of the ABC
> Department Store. Bessie is suspicious of Tillie
> and thinks she saw Tillie put a record under
> her coat. Bessie follows Tillie to the ladies'
> room where she refuses to let Tillie exit until
> she confesses to the theft. Bessie has com-
> mitted the offense of unlawful restraint.

Many states, trying to protect merchants from shoplifting losses, specifically provide that a merchant or an
employee who reasonably believes that a person has
wrongfully taken, or is about to wrongfully take, merchandise from the merchant's place of business may,
without committing the offense of unlawful restraint,
detain the suspect for a reasonable time in a reasonable
manner for the purpose of determining the ownership of
the merchandise.

> *Example*
> A female store detective observes Helen, at
> the phonograph record counter, place some-

thing resembling a record under her coat and walk toward the store exit. In some states, by statute, the detective (or other store employees) may detain Helen and inquire about the object and its ownership.

Despite such statutory authorization, merchants are wary about exercising it for fear of false arrest suits. Generally they do not attempt any detention unless the person's conduct warrants an arrest for theft. In other words, unless the person is seen taking and concealing an unpurchased article, no detention is attempted. Some merchants even delay arrest until the taker has left the store; in that way the taker is deprived of any innocent explanation for his conduct. But whenever a person's conduct shows a provable intent to steal, a merchant or his store detective is legally justified in arresting that person as a shoplifter and having him prosecuted for the crime of theft.

BATTERY AND ASSAULT

A battery occurs when a person, by any means, knowingly and unlawfully touches another person in an insulting or provoking manner. Some statutes do not require the touching to be insulting or provoking in nature, as long as the victim has suffered bodily harm.

Examples

1. Joe, a student, disagreed with his college instructor's lecture and noted his dissent by spitting in the instructor's face. Joe has committed a battery.
2. Harry and Pete arrived in a movie house balcony at the same time from different directions. One seat was available and

Harry, in order to stake claim to the seat, aggressively pushed Pete out of the way. Harry has committed a battery.

In many jurisdictions, there is an increased penalty for battery when the offender uses a deadly weapon, is masked or hooded, or chooses a member of a particularly designated class of persons for his victim, such as police officers or teachers. And when the offender, in committing a battery, causes permanent disability or disfigurement to his victim, a more serious penalty is provided. Such a degree of battery is often called "mayhem."

An assault occurs when a person, without lawful authority, does anything that places another person in reasonable apprehension of receiving a battery. An assault does not involve a touching. If touching occurs, the offense is a battery.

Examples

1. Jim, a husky six-footer, got into an argument at a party with another guest, jockey-sized Ron. Jim took a punch at Ron, but because of his myopia (of which Ron was not aware) he missed by a foot. Other guests restrained Jim from any further action. Jim is guilty of assault. Had he hit Ron, he would have committed a battery.
2. Joe, enraged at Bill, backed him against a wall and fired a loaded pistol at him. The pistol jammed and did not fire. Joe is guilty of attempted murder, as discussed in another section of this book. But he is also guilty of assault because he put Bill in reasonable apprehension of receiving a battery.

The trend in recent years, however, has been to remove [t]he stigma of criminality from all forms of sexual conduct [pe]rformed in privacy between consenting adults. Homo-[se]xuality, for instance, has been removed from the [c]riminal statutes in at least one state (Illinois), but only [w]hen the conduct is mutually consented to, is done in [p]rivate, and does not involve a young person with an [o]lder one.

Prostitution and Related Offenses

Prostitution was not a common law crime, although keeping a house of prostitution was. The keeping of a bawdy house was thought to corrupt public morals, but the act of prostitution was not viewed as seriously. Today, however, both kinds of conduct are generally unlawful.

Some states have also made it an offense to solicit or to patronize a prostitute. Outlawed, too, are certain kinds of related conduct, involving a third party who lives off the proceeds of prostitution such as "solicitation for a prostitute," "pandering" or "pimping." Such related offenses commonly involve organized crime and are labeled "commercialized vice."

The Federal White Slave Act

A federal statute, passed by Congress in 1910, but amended to some extent thereafter, makes it a crime

> "to knowingly transport in interstate or foreign commerce, or in the District of Columbia or in any Territory or Possession of the United States, any woman or girl for the purpose of prostitution or debauchery, or for any other immoral purpose, or with the intent and purpose to induce, entice, or compel her to become a prostitute or to give herself up to debauchery, or to engage in any other immoral practice."

As in the case of battery, an assault by a masked or hooded offender, or one who uses a deadly weapon, or an assault against a member of a particular class of persons, often calls for a greater penalty than simple assault.

SEX OFFENSES

Forcible Rape

Rape was originally defined as unlawful sexual intercourse with a female "by force and against her will." Although many earlier cases held that a woman was required to resist "to the utmost," submission out of fear of violence is now generally held to constitute rape.

An early statute in England declared that intercourse with a child under ten years of age was also rape, regardless of "consent." What about a case in which a female is so drunk that she is incapable of consenting? In such a situation, the act is presumed to be without her consent and therefore rape. Modern statutes generally provide that rape is committed whenever the victim is unconscious (as from drink or drugs), or is so mentally deranged or deficient that she cannot effectively give consent to the act of intercourse.

Since the crime of rape requires that the sexual act be unlawful, a married man could not be guilty of "raping" his wife. Marriage rendered the act lawful. It is interesting to note, however, that if a married man compelled his wife to have intercourse with another man, the husband could be found guilty of rape. His conduct renders him an "accessory" to the rape and therefore guilty of the crime itself. Under a similar line of reasoning, a woman might be convicted of raping another woman.

Intercourse, within the meaning of rape, consists of any

penetration, however slight, of the female sex organ by the male sex organ, regardless of whether or not the organ was erect. Thus, impotency is no defense for rape. Moreover, an emission is not required as an element of the crime.

Sex Offenses against Children

Statutory Rape

In an effort to protect children from sexual conduct involving older persons, various legislatures have enacted separate child sex offense statutes. One is the crime of "statutory rape," which consists of sexual intercourse with a female under a certain age, usually 16, regardless of whether or not she consents. Believing that a girl is over the specified age is generally not a defense, regardless of the reasonableness of the belief. But there are a few court decisions and statutory provisions to the contrary.

Indecent Liberties and Contributing to Sexual Delinquency

Modern legislation, in a further effort to protect the young, has established several additional sex offenses. One is "indecent liberties with a child"; another is "contributing to the sexual delinquency of a child." The two offenses consist essentially of any lewd fondling for the purpose of arousing the sexual desires of either the male or the female under the specified age, which is usually 16.

Incest

Another offense, also intended for the protection of the young, is "incest." The classic example is sexual intercourse by a father with his daughter. The offense has long been extended to include mothers and sons, brothers and sisters and, in some states, certain other blood relationships.

Adultery and Fornication

Adultery is sexual intercourse bet[ween] [one married] person and another person other than [his or her spouse.] For divorce purposes, one "sneak" exper[ience is enough.] In most jurisdiction, however, in order fo[r it to con]stitute a crime, the parties' behavior must [be a scandal] to others: the adulterous conduct must [be "open and] notorious."

Fornication generally consists of cohabit[ation and] sexual intercourse between unmarried persons [under cir]cumstances in which their behavior is well [known to] others: in other words, "open and notorious." Th[e penalty] for fornication is less than that for adultery. In som[e states,] Louisiana for one, there are no such crimes as adulte[ry or] fornication. The same is also generally true in fo[reign] countries.

Bigamy

A married person who marries a second person commi[ts] bigamy. The crime can also be committed by a single person if he or she marries someone he or she knows to be still married to another. In some states, a defense to a charge of bigamy is that the accused reasonably believed the prior marriage had been legally dissolved or that the previous spouse was dead.

Deviate Sexual Conduct

In the past, almost any sexual gratification derived from hetero-sexual intimacies other than the one with the potential of reproduction (organ-to-organ intercourse) was considered a crime. Any oral-genital contact, even between husband and wife in the privacy of their home, was unlawful. So was any sexual activity between members of the same sex. And, most certainly, any human-animal sexual contact was prohibited and severly punishable.

The White Slave Act, also known as the Mann Act because it was introduced as a bill by Representative James R. Mann, was intended to discourge the "commercial vice" of traffic in women for monetary gain. It has been interpreted, however, to cover the transportation of a woman across a state line for the purpose of becoming the concubine or mistress of the transporter; so, as interpreted by the courts, the transportation need not be for commercial gain. All that is required is transportation for an "immoral purpose" or an "immoral practice," depending upon how those terms may be interpreted in any given situation. However, the act is rarely enforced except in cases of commercialized vice.

Public Annoyance

Exhibitionism

According to common law, any "obscene" or "indecent" act of a public nature was punishable as a crime because of its injurious effect upon "public morality." Under that principle, a person could be punished criminally for "indecently" exposing his or her sexual organs in public, the usual motivation being the sexual gratification of the exhibitor. Today, such conduct is made criminal by specific ordinances or statutes. Prosecutions for such conduct may be initiated under some general ordinance or statute, such as that prohibiting "disorderly conduct." Disorderly conduct is usually defined in legislative enactments as conduct that alarms or disturbs another person and thus provokes a breach of the peace.

Window Peeping

Common law prosecutions were attempted against "window peepers" or "Peeping Toms" when their actions

affected "public morality," but the courts were reluctant
to classify such conduct within that category. On the other
hand, there has been considerable difficulty whenever
attempts have been made to draft legislation dealing
specifically with conduct of that nature. Constitutional
due process guarantees against legislative "vagueness" or
"indefiniteness" have presented problems of an almost
insurmountable nature.

If window peeping were done in such a way as to
provoke a "breach of the peace," disorderly conduct might
be involved. But, ordinarily, a window peeper indulges in
his conduct in secrecy and darkness.

About as far as legislators can go is to make it an
offense to enter upon the property of another and to look
into a dwelling for a "lewd and unlawful purpose." But,
here again, it is difficult to prove that purpose. In any
event, the individual who enters upon the property of
another without authority is subject to another and more
easily established offense—trespass.

Because of the frequent attempts by home owners to
shoot and kill window peepers, it is important to stress
that there is no legal justification for using a lethal force
to discourage such conduct or to apprehend the offender,
even when the peeping may involve trespass. Lethal force
is justifiable only to prevent a serious felony (for example,
burglary) or to apprehend a felon of that type.

Anonymous Telephone Calls

One of the most annoying, though generally harmless,
acts of misconduct is the anonymous telephone call that is
usually motivated by the need for sexual gratification. The
caller may do no more than telephone a female for the
purpose of hearing her voice, without saying anything
himself. But such a caller often uses obscene language or
makes indecent proposals to her.

The legal problem of anonymous telephone calls is usually dealt with in state statutes governing the general use of telephones, rather than in state criminal law provisions. Such statutes generally prohibit, among other things, the use of language that is "obscene, lewd or immoral, with the intent to offend another person." A federal statute also makes it an offense to use the telephone in that manner. Telephone companies are very cooperative in the investigation of such calls, and willingly take the necessary measures to protect the recipient from further annoyance.

Chapter 2

Crimes Against Property

THEFT AND RELATED OFFENSES

Larceny

The earliest crime established by common law to discourage theft was larceny. It consisted of the "taking and carrying away" of the "personal property" of another, with "intent to steal" (i.e., to "permanently deprive" another of his property). If any of these elements was missing in a particular case, the accused could not be found guilty of larceny.

One of the early difficulties in larceny prosecutions occurred when the owner of the property had relinquished possession to another person who proceeded to convert it to his own use, or otherwise to dispose of it. For instance, if John asked Sam to lend him his horse to go to town, and on the way John sold the horse, there could be no larceny because the element of "taking" was not present.

Another problem in early larceny cases was establishing the required element of "carrying away." For instance, assuming a person picked up a piece of personal property belonging to someone else, with the express intent to steal it, how far did he have to go with it for his action to amount to "carrying away"? An additional difficulty, and one that is inherently a part of larceny cases, centered around proving an "intent to steal." The entire issue can be best illustrated, perhaps, by the following hypothetical case, based upon a shoplifting situation:

While in a department store, Jane picks up a pair of hose. Instead of walking toward the sales person on duty, she walks to the opposite end of the counter and in the direction of the store exit. Meanwhile, she is carrying the hose folded in her hand. As she nears the exit, a store detective arrests her for theft (or larceny, depending upon the category into which shoplifting falls in the particular state). Have the required elements been established?

Although the "taking" and "the carrying away" of personal property of another (the store) may seem clear enough, the store may be hard pressed to prove the "intent to steal." Jane may claim she was only taking and carrying away the hose so she could examine them in the daylight near the exit. What proof could the store offer to establish a different intent?

Now consider a slightly different situation:

On the windowed and well-lighted second floor of a department store, Joyce picks up a sweater. Although several sales persons are nearby to handle a sales transaction, Joyce walks to a stairway and heads for the alley exit. A store detective catches her. In this case, there is good reason to believe that Joyce intended to steal the sweater.

As previously pointed out, store detectives generally wait until a person has put some object into a purse or otherwise concealed it before taking any action; or else they wait until the unpaid merchandise has been taken outside the store. But such delayed action is only a precaution to nullify a possible false explanation of

innocent purpose. In short, if ample evidence of "intent
to steal" exists while the taker is still on the premises, there
is no legal need to wait for the taker's departure from the
store before detaining or arresting him.

Larceny by Bailee and Embezzlement

In an effort to plug up a loophole in the original common
law crime of larceny, and in order to be able to successfully prosecute the person who converts personal property
to his own use after having received possession or control
of it from the owner, the English Parliament and early
American Legislatures created the new crimes of "larceny
by bailee" and "embezzlement."

Examples
1. Bill is given a package of merchandise to
   deliver to Ed. Bill, considered the "bailee,"
   sells it to Leo, and pockets the proceeds.
   Bill has committed "larceny by bailee."
2. Art, a bankteller, pockets $500 which he
   received for deposit. He has committed
   "embezzlement."

False Pretenses and Confidence Games

Another early effort to amend the deficiency in the
original definition of larceny was the creation of the
offense of obtaining money or property under "false pretenses" or by means of a "confidence game." The former
was usually a misdemeanor; the latter was usually a felony.

Examples
1. Jerry shows Ann a diamond ring which he
   says is solid gold. He offers to sell it for
   $300. Ann buys it and later discovers that
   the ring is gold-plated and that the alleged
   "diamond" is nothing but a piece of ordinary

glass. At the time of the transaction, Jerry knew, of course, that his representation was false. He is guilty of the crime of "false pretenses."

2. Henry meets a rich widow, dates her several times, then tells her he knows how he can double her money within sixty days by investing it in an oil drilling operation in Alaska. He induces her to make a large check payable to him in order to simplify the investment transaction. But Henry actually has made no arrangements for such an investment. He leaves town several days after cashing the check, buys a boat with the money and leaves for South America. Henry is guilty of a "confidence game." He fooled his victim after having gained her confidence.

Modern Theft Legislation

Present legislation is doing away with the various theft crimes that in the past have had a variety of labels and created problems of interpretation. The 1961 Illinois Criminal Code exemplifies each new legislation.

At one time there were seventy-four separate provisions in the Illinois statutes dealing with theft. Most of them were enacted over many years for the purpose of plugging the loopholes in preceding statutes; now there is one provision for "theft" that covers almost all of the situations which were the basis for the multitude of earlier enactments, including the crime of "receiving stolen property." The Illinois Code simply states that a person commits theft when he knowingly obtains or exerts unauthorized control over another person's property or obtains control by deception or threats, or when he receives stolen property or receives such property under circumstances which would reasonably indicate it was stolen, when he intends to deprive the owner permanently of the use or benefit of the property.

The punishment for the theft under common law larceny was usually of two grades, based upon the monetary value of the object taken. Any larceny under $15 was labeled "petit larceny"; over that amount it was termed "grand larceny." Petit larceny was considered a misdemeanor, punishable by a jail sentence of up to one year. Grand larceny was considered a felony, punishable by a penitentiary sentence of one year or more. Today, the dividing line between petit larceny and grand larceny is usually set at a larger amount, such as $100 or $150, which merely reflects monetary inflation.

Another variant punishment occurs when the theft is from the person of another without his knowledge, i.e., pickpocketing. In such instances, in deference to possible physical danger to the victim, the statutory penalty is generally more severe than in stealing other than from the person.

Robbery

Robbery is generally defined as the taking of money or personal property from the person of another by force or by threat of force.

Example

> Moe grabs Jack around the neck and removes his wallet.

Robbery committed while the offender is armed is called "armed robbery" in some states. Even if not given that designation, however, the penalty for robbery while armed is greater than for ordinary "strong-arm" robbery.

Example

> Using a gun, Phil demands and receives Bob's wallet.

Burglary

Burglary under common law consisted of "breaking and entering" into the "dwelling house" of another "in the night time" with the "intent to steal." Many early cases created the question of what constitutes "breaking." Suppose a door were slightly ajar and the would-be thief merely shoved it far enough to squeeze his body through. Suppose he hid in a trunk that was labeled for delivery into a home, and gained entry in that way. Would such cases constitute "breaking"?

The meaning of "dwelling house" also presented a problem. Suppose the building were a summer home or cottage and the breaking and entering occurred in the winter, when it was unoccupied and boarded up. Would such a building be considered a "dwelling house"? Even the meaning of "night time" caused trouble when the act occurred at twilight.

Those and similar problems are gradually being resolved by legislation which simply states that a person commits burglary when, without authority, he knowingly enters, or without authority remains within, a building, housetrailer, watercraft, aircraft, railroad car, or any part of such places, with intent to commit a felony or theft. Such legislation eliminates the controversies over the meanings of "breaking and entering," "dwelling house," and "night time."

The difficulty of establishing in all cases the element of "intent" remains, but it has been and will continue to be a problem as long as we adhere to the fundamentally desirable concept that no one should be punished for an offense as serious as burglary unless he *intended* to do wrong. Otherwise, any person who entered a building or any other structure by mistake could be convicted of burglary.

Because of its danger to life and limb, burglary, like

robbery, carries a stiffer penalty than theft without dangerous circumstances.

Forgery

Forgery occurs when a person knowingly makes, alters, issues, delivers, or possesses with intent to issue or to deliver any document capable of defrauding and designed to defraud another person.

Examples

1. John wrote a check payable to himself and signed it with a fictitious name. He endorsed the check and cashed it at the local tavern. John is guilty of forgery.
2. Bill owed Pete $90 and sent him a $9 check in partial payment. Pete knew Bill had plenty in the bank so he added an extra zero and changed the "nine" to "ninety" before cashing it. Pete is guilty of forgery.
3. Harry is planning a business trip abroad. His friend Tom, a bank official, issues a letter of credit from his bank stating that Harry has $100,000 credit with the bank, when in fact he has no such credit. Harry carries Tom's letter with him to use in case he comes across a favorable business deal requiring a showing of his financial responsibilities. Under some state laws, both Harry and Tom are guilty of forgery.

Interstate Theft

Several federal statutes prohibit and prescribe punishment for the interstate transportation of stolen property and for the theft of property being transported from one state to another. The authorization for such federal legis-

lation is derived from the constitutional power of Congress
to regulate interstate commerce.

Examples
1. Bob steals an automobile in State A and
   drives it into State B. In addition to committing the state offense of theft, Bob has
   committed a federal crime.
2. A television manufacturer in State A ships
   by truck or rail a number of television sets
   to a dealer in State B. On the way, Al and
   Phil steal several of the sets. They have
   committed a federal offense.

A theft of property in interstate shipment, in violation
of federal law, is punishable in the courts of the state in
which it occurred. Ordinarily, however, the charge is
brought and tried in the federal courts alone.

Federal Theft

A theft of property belonging to the United States Government may be punished by the state within which it
occurs as well as by the federal government, but the state
authorities usually relinquish their right to prosecute. The
same procedure usually prevails for embezzlements from
national banks and from other federally insured corpora-
tions and organizations, and also for burglaries and robberies committed within such institutions.

Misprision of Felony and Compounding a Crime

Along with theft it is appropriate to discuss the little
known, yet very important, offenses known as "misprision
of felony" and "compounding a crime." The nature of
these similar offenses may be best described by quoting
from both a federal statute, "misprision of felony," and a
state statute, "compounding a crime."

The federal statute, under the title of "Misprision of Felony," provides that

> "Whoever, having knowledge of the actual commission of a felony conceals and does not as soon as possible make known the same to some judge or other person in civil or military authority under the United States, shall be fined not more than $500 or imprisoned not more than three years, or both."

Examples

1. Jack knows that Mark has stolen property over $100 in value from a Navy shipyard. If Jack fails to report the matter, he is guilty of misprision of felony.
2. Art, a bank president of a national bank, knows that a teller in the bank has embezzled over $100. If Art does not report it, he commits misprision of felony.

The states have not been as concerned as the federal government about a person who knows that another person has committed a felony and does not report it. Unless the person with such knowledge takes some affirmative action to hide the crime or to assist the felon to escape, he does not violate a state law. About as far as the states have been willing to go is to create the crime of "compounding a crime."

The state statutory offense of "compounding a crime" is sometimes phrased as follows: "A person compounds a crime when he receives or offers to another any consideration for a promise not to prosecute or aid in the prosecution of an offender."

Example

Bill steals or embezzles $5,000 from his employer. Bill's father offers $1,000 in restitution, upon the employer's promise not to initiate a prosecution against Bill. Bill's father is guilty of "compounding a crime" by reason of his offer; and, if the employer accepts the restitution money, he, too, is guilty of that offense.

It should be pointed out, however, that after a prosecution has been initiated a court may withhold punishment for a guilty plea if the thief or someone on his behalf agrees to make, and makes, restitution that is satisfactory to the victim.

PROPERTY DAMAGE AND INTRUSIONS

Arson and Criminal Damage

Of all the acts directed at damage to property, the most serious is the crime of arson. A modern version of the definition of arson (as in Illinois) provides that a person commits arson when, by fire or explosion, he knowingly damages any real property, or any personal property having a value of $150 or more, of another person without his consent; or, with intent to defraud an insurer, damages any property or any personal property having a value of $150 or more.

Property of another, under that definition of arson, means a building or other property, whether real or personal, in which a person other than the offender has an interest which the offender has no authority to defeat or impair, even though the offender may also have an interest in the building or property. This provision avoids the uncertainties of the old, common law definition of arson. There is now no need to determine if "burning" occurred; it is sufficient if "damage" has been caused by either explosion or fire. The provision also covers the burning of one's own property when the purpose is to defraud an insurer. Under common law, the property had to be another person's dwelling.

The figure of $150 mentioned in the definition of arson, regardless of whether the statute involves one's own property of that of someone else, could be set at any figure selected by the legislature. The monetary specification only draws the line between the penalty designations for felony and misdemeanor.

Generally, the penalty for arson is a severe one. If death occurs because of arson—or, rather, if death can be considered to be a result of the act and the circumstances surrounding it—the offender is guilty of felony-murder.

Other kinds of intentional, criminal damage to another person's property are also punishable, but less severely than is arson. Even when fire or explosion is used to damage personal property other than a building, the conduct may be considered a misdemeanor, subject to appropriate punishment, if the value of the property is under the specified statutory amount. And the offense of criminal damage to personal property may include injuries to domestic animals. Some legislatures have described lesser forms of criminal damage to property as "malicious mischief." Presently, though, a number of legislatures have made it a felony to intentionally damage school property by fire or explosive.

Trespass

A person who enters upon the land of another, after receiving, immediately prior to such entry, notice from the owner or occupant that entry is forbidden, commits the offense of trespass. A trespass is also committed whenever a person remains on the land of another after receiving notice to depart. The required notice may be oral or in writing. If in writing, it must be conspicuously posted or exhibited, and particularly at the main entrance or at points where access seems available.

Chapter 3

Offenses Affecting Public Morals, Health, Safety and Welfare

OBSCENITY

The First Amendment to the Constitution of the United States guarantees freedom of speech and freedom of the press, but both freedoms have been held by the courts not to include the protection of obscenity. Because obscenity is not constitutionally protected, the various legislatures may make it a crime to sell, publish, disseminate, or possess with intent to disseminate, any obscene picture or writing. Similarly, it is a crime to perform, direct, produce, or promote an obscene act or performance. But no one can be criminally liable for permitting obscenity within the privacy of his home: the Supreme Court of the United States has held that a person has a constitutional right to possess, read, or look at whatever he desires.

Determining Obscenity

To determine whether or not a particular picture, writing or performance is obscene, and thus subject to legal prohibitions, the following tests must be applied:

(a) Does most (the "dominant theme") of the material, considered in its entirety ("taken as a whole"), appeal to a morbid or shameful ("prurient") interest in nudity, sex, or excretion?

(b) In determining the principal design, or dominate theme, of the material in accordance with point (a), the material must be examined through the viewpoint of an "average person," based upon "contemporary community standards."

(c) "Contemporary community standards," as used in point (b), generally means national standards for ascertaining whether or not the material in question is "patently offensive."

(d) Even if the material is objectionable under the guidelines of (a), (b), and (c), it must also be "utterly without any redeeming social, literary, historical, scientific, or other value." When difficulty arises over determining whether or not there is any "redeeming value," the method used in advertising or exploiting the material may be examined. If the material is exploited or advertised to stress its lewd or lascivious aspects, it is considered to be without redeeming importance. However, if advertising or exploiting stresses the purported redeeming nature of the material, it could be considered to have redeeming social importance and therefore not to be obscene.

Here are some illustrations of the application of the above guidelines for testing obscenity:

1. A motion picture used for the education of a class of future parents is seized by the police. It contains numerous scenes of nude women. Although the film may appeal to an interest in sex or nudity, that interest is neither shameful nor morbid and is therefore not obscene.

2. A local bookstore is selling an 18th-century English novel detailing the sex life of a prominent female. The book may not be obscene. Although the primary interest of the book is a morbid interest in sex, it may contain redeeming historical or literary merit. The book may be well-written and it may accurately elucidate the morality of a segment of society in an historical period in England.

3. The police seize a photogragh that a man is offering for sale to a youth in which a man and woman are portrayed in the nude in an act of sexual intercourse. The photograph is considered obscene. It appeals to a morbid or shameful interest in sex and nudity, and has no redeeming merit.

In order to convict a person of the offense of obscenity, it must be shown that he knew the nature of the obscene material. Showing such knowledge is called proof of "scienter." It is rarely proved directly—that is, by an admission of the charged person that he knew the nature of the obscene material. Most often, "scienter" is shown circumstantially from the facts involved in the case. The following factual examples show an existence of "scienter."

1. A bookseller keeps a substantial stock of obscene books in a separate section of his store. The books were supplied by a wholesale firm that deals exclusively in obscene books. The bookseller had visited the wholesale firm on many occasions and had purchased its books. Such circumstances establish his knowledge that the books were obscene.

2. Hugh was the managing partner of an enterprise that specialized in books of a salacious character. He prepared the newspaper advertising for the books. He admitted that he knew they could not be sent through the mails because of the nature of their subject matter. Proof of knowledge of the obscene nature of the books is thereby established.

3. The books in question were printed on cheap paper and contained obscene cover pictures. They were also priced high and an excessive profit resulted. Knowledge of the obscene character of the books is thereby established.

4. The sales price of the small paperback books was $4.50 each. The books were kept by the defendant next to the cash register. The covers of the books were themselves "obscene and offensive," and bore the warning "Adults Only." Here, too, the required element of knowledge is present.

The legal procedures for determining whether or not a motion picture is obscene differ from those relating to books and art. Only motion pictures may be subject to "prior restraint" (censorship) as a condition to being licensed for showing. Usually, an arrest for obscenity is made only after the publication or performance of the alleged obscene material. The exception is pre-release censorship, or "prior restraint," on motion pictures. This principle has been approved by the Supreme Court of the United States.

A governmental body may therefore require submission of motion pictures in advance of exhibition before licensing the film for showing, but the Supreme Court has stated that prior restraint procedures must be accompanied by certain safeguards: (a) the burden of proving a film obscene rests upon the governmental agency; (b) the government may not finally determine that a film is obscene without court approval which is done by obtaining an injunction against the showing of the film; and (c) both the government's administrative procedures and the court's judicial procedures must allow for a speedy final determination about whether or not the showing of the film may be prohibited on the ground of obscenity.

When and where a motion picture is licensed by a governmental board, the motion picture, its distributor and its exhibitor are all protected from prosecution under the criminal law for obscenity, and the police department may not make an arrest based upon its independent judgment that the motion picture is obscene.

Following the suggestion of some members of the Supreme Court, a few jurisdictions have abandoned full censorship of films in favor of a limited form of "prior restraint," often referred to as "classification" of films. Under a "classification" procedure, only those films which are to be shown to audiences that include children need to be licensed. The procedural safeguard requirements are the same as those for full censorship. It is not to be confused, however, with the "self-regulation" labeling of films by the Motion Picture Association of America.

Enforcement of Obscenity Laws

Parents are often frustrated by the seemingly open sale of "filthy" books and the exhibition of "dirty" films. As a practical matter, there is little law enforcement officials can do about borderline films and literature. The Supreme Court's definition of obscenity excludes materials which have the "slightest" amount of "redeeming social, literary, historical, or esthetic value," no matter how prurient its over-all appeal may be. If 90 percent of the appeal were to a "prurient" interest, the court would not classify the book or film as obscene if the other 10 percent of its appeal were to a social, literary, historical, or esthetic interest. How, then, can a beautifully filmed and artistically directed pornographic movie ever be obscene? And how can a magazine full of suggestive nudity be obscene when it includes a quality article on photography or on human anatomy? Also note that the Supreme Court's definition of obscenity does not include violence. Therefore, works with explicit scenes of "blood and gore" are not covered by the obscenity prohibitions, a phenomenon which is contrary to the laws in most other countries.

The Supreme Court has also laid down costly and difficult procedural requirements for the censorship of films which inhibit most states and municipalities from taking any legal action. The Court has also set forth special requirements for the issuance and execution of search warrants for obscene material which make it more difficult to seize such material than any other contraband. The public, frustrated by what it considers law enforcement inaction or indifference, is mostly unaware of the technical prohibitions on law enforcement officers who may take action only within the constitutional framework of the law as interpreted by the Supreme Court.

ABORTION

An illegal abortion occurs when a person, without legal justification, uses any instrument, or administers any medicine, drug or other substance, with the intent to cause the rejection or removal of a fetus from a pregnant female. It is punishable as a felony. If death occurs as a consequence, the offense becomes a felony-murder.

In most states, the only legal justification for an abortion is the preservation of the life of the pregnant woman, although a few jurisdictions, such as the District of Columbia, permit abortions to be performed when necessary to preserve the health of the pregnant woman. The modern

In most states, the only legal justification for an abortion laws. Within the past several years, a few states (e.g., Colorado and North Carolina) have enacted statutes which legalize abortions, when performed by a licensed physician in a hospital for the following reasons: (a) when abortion is medically advisable because the fetus would be born with a grave and irremediable physical or mental defect; (b) when the pregnancy is the result of a forcible rape or incest.

Example

A pregnant woman receives medication (e.g., Thalidomide) to relieve her discomfort, but the medical profession subsequently ascertains that a frequent "side effect" of the medication is the production of horrible physical deformities in the child (e.g., no limbs). An abortion would be permissible.

Continuing the trend toward liberalization, some state courts have even held conventional abortion laws unconstitutional on grounds of violation of the right to privacy and vagueness in the phraseology of the laws.

In most jurisdictions, a person can be convicted of an attempted abortion even though the woman was not in fact pregnant.

Example

Milly woke up one morning with a stomach ache. She erroneously decided that she was pregnant and told her boy friend of her concern. They went to a one-time physician who previously had lost his license for performing an illegal abortion. He inserted a surgical device in her vagina and announced that the abortion was successful. On learning of the foregoing, Milly's parents reported the incident to the police. In most jurisdictions the doctor would be guilty of attempted illegal abortion. The fact that Milly was not pregnant would be no defense against the charges.

The wording of some state statutes abolishes the distinction between abortion and attempted abortion. The crime of abortion covers both. Such a statute may read, in part, as follows:

"It shall not be necessary in order to commit abortion that such woman be pregnant, or if pregnant, that a miscarriage be in fact accomplished."

GAMBLING

In all but a few states, many different types of conduct constitute the offense of gambling. The most common are the following.

Wagering by Participant

Gambling is a game of chance or skill played for money or for other things of value.

Example

> Several men play poker for stakes of $1.00 limit every Friday night at a local club. Their conduct constitutes unlawful gambling. However, when it is a simple social event, not involving profit for the sponsoring individual or for the club itself, rarely is there any police interference.

Many states provide for an exemption from their gambling laws for the awarding of prizes or compensation to the actual contestants in a bona fide contest of skill, speed, strength or endurance.

Example

> A country club stages a professional golf tournament. The winner is to receive $10,000. Other professional golfers who finish high in the tournament standings are to receive lesser sums as compensation. The tournament is not a gambling activity.

Wagering by Bystander

It is gambling for a person to make a wager on any game, contest or other event involving persons other than himself.

Example

> Several baseball fans sitting in the bleachers at a ball park bet on various aspects of the baseball game: that is, on whether the next pitch will be a ball or a strike, on whether or

not the batter will get on base, on whether or not the pitcher will complete the game. Such betting is unlawful gambling activity.

Exempted from the foregoing prohibition against by-stander gambling are insurance agreements to compensate for losses that result from fire, storms and death. Another usual exemption is the awarding of prizes or compensation to owners of animals or vehicles that are entered in a bona fide contest for the determination of skill, speed, strength or endurance. By a considerable stretch of judicial reasoning, pari mutuel betting has been held valid even in states where the constitutions prescribe prohibitions against gambling.

Possession of Gambling Devices

A gambling offense occurs in most states when a person operates, keeps, owns, uses, purchases, exhibits, rents, sells, bargains for the sale or lease of, manufactures, or distributes any gambling device. A common statutory definition of a "gambling device" is: any clock, tape machine, slot machine, or other machine or device for the reception of money or other thing of value on chance or skill or upon the action of which money or other thing of value is staked, hazarded, bet, won or lost; or any mechanism, furniture, fixture, equipment or other device designed primarily for use in a gambling place. A "gambling device" does not ordinarily include:

> (a) a coin-operated mechanical device played for amusement that rewards the player with the right to replay and that is constructed or devised to make the operation of the device depend, in part, on the skill of the player, and that does not return to the player money, property, or the right to receive money or property; and

(b) vending machines that return full and adequate value for the money invested, with no element of chance or hazard.

Examples

1. A country club has several slot machines. The proceeds from these machines are used to purchase gifts for veterans at the local V.A. Hospital. However worthy the cause may be, the machines are gambling devices, prohibited by law.

2. A country club has a mechanical bowling machine and a candy bar vending machine (which sometimes malfunctions and gives two candy bars for the price of one). The machines are not gambling devices.

Bookmaking

The offense of gambling occurs when a person owns or has any book, instrument, or apparatus that records or registers bets or wagers, or when a person knowingly holds any money that he has received as the result of a bet or wager. Such activity is called "bookmaking."

Example

Sam, the proprietor of Sam's Cigar Store, takes wagers at his store for the gambling "syndicate." Sam records these wagers in a ledger. He is guilty of gambling.

Poolselling

The offense of gambling also occurs when a person sells pools on the result of any game or contest of skill or chance, political nomination, appointment or election.

Example

Ten or more members of the steno pool at an office each contribute $1.00 to the Kentucky Derby pot. Each girl draws a slip of paper from a bowl, containing the names of all the horses entered in the race. The girl who has the slip with the name of the winning horse on it wins the money in the pot. All the girls have committed the offense of gambling. Such an infraction of the law, however, is rarely prosecuted.

Lottery

The offense of gambling also occurs when a person sets up or promotes any lottery, or sells, offers to sell, or transfers any ticket or share in any lottery. A "lottery" is any scheme or procedure in which one or more prizes are distributed by chance among persons who have paid or promised consideration for a chance to win the prizes, regardless of whether the scheme or procedure is a raffle, gift, or sale, or is called by some other name. Supermarket and gas station promotional games are usually exempted by statute or court decision on the theory that a purchase of goods is not required in order for a person to obtain a chance or ticket.

Examples

1. The local church runs a bingo game, selling bingo cards for $1.00 each per game. Valuable prizes are awarded to the winner. The profits from the game go toward missionary and other charitable work. The activity is unlawful gambling in most states.
2. The local supermarket gives a stamp containing a picture of a baseball player to each

customer and person who comes in the store and asks for one. When the recipient collects five stamps bearing the pictures of five different players, he receives $100 in cash. In most jurisdictions, it would not be considered an unlawful lottery.

Numbers, Policy and Bolita

Numbers, policy and bolita are illegal because they involve the payment of a sum of money for the chance to win a greater sum of money.

Example

Bill sells tickets containing four numbers each for the "Wheel of Fortune" game. After the tickets are sold, Bill spins his roulette-type wheel four times. The holder of the ticket containing the four numbers selected by the wheel is awarded one half of the total funds collected by Bill from the sale of the tickets. It is an unlawful gambling activity.

Gambling Places

The offense of keeping a gambling place occurs when a person knowingly permits any premises or property owned or occupied by him or under his control to be used as a gambling place. A common statutory definition of a "gambling place" includes any real estate, vehicle, boat or any other property that is used for the purpose of gambling.

Some states, in addition to penalizing a keeper of a gambling place, move against the gambling place itself as a "nuisance" under state law. If declared by a court to be a nuisance, the building in which gambling has occurred may be ordered closed ("padlocked") for a period of time, perhaps as long as a year. Some states also provide for the forfeiture of the liquor licenses of a tavern where gambling occurs and for the court sale of a gambling place to pay any unsatisfied fine.

Syndicated Gambling

In a special effort to suppress gambling that is controlled by organized crime syndicates, a few states have enacted "syndicated gambling" laws that prescribe a considerably greater penalty whenever the nature of the gambling clearly indicates a large scale operation. That may be based upon the amount and the number of the bets.

Miscellaneous Gambling Laws

Most jurisdictions have statutory provisions that provide for the forfeiture of gambling funds confiscated in a lawful search and seizure. The gambling funds that are seized are usually authorized by statute to be forfeited to the treasury of the state, county or municipality, and the gambling devices that are seized are usually authorized to be destroyed by the local law enforcement authorities. Motor vehicles used in gambling operations are also subject to confiscation.

> *Example*
>
> Acting with a proper search warrant, the police raid the back room of Joe's Cigar Store. A poker game is in progress and two slot machines are being played. After Joe's conviction for being the keeper of a gambling place, the money used in the poker game and in the slot machines is forfeited to the county treasury and the machines are destroyed.

Gambling agreements are not enforceable by court proceedings, since they are considered "contracts contrary to public policy."

Example

Sam places a bet with Bill, a bookmaker, on a football game. Sam wins, but Bill does not pay off. Sam cannot sue Bill for the money due him.

Federal Prohibitions

In 1950, as a result of the hearings conducted by a Special Senate Committee to Investigate Organized Crime in Interstate Commerce, under the Chairmanship of the late Senator Estes Kefauver, Congress began to consider various ways in which effective Congressional assistance could be given to the states in the effort to suppress illegal gambling. The first development, in 1959, was the enactment of a statute prohibiting the interstate transportation of gambling devices. Congress subsequently prohibited the interstate transportation of wagering "paraphernalia" and wagering "information."

NARCOTIC DRUGS

The definition of "narcotics" in most states is similar to the federal law definition. Narcotic drugs usually include opium, insonipecaine, and coca leaves, whether produced directly or indirectly by extraction of substances of vegetable origin, or independently by means of chemical synthesis. Also included are any other substances which are chemically identical to such drugs. Morphine, codeine, and heroin are derivatives of opium. Cocaine is derived from coca leaves.

Although not a narcotic drug in the scientific sense, for the purpose of criminal law marijuana is treated as one. Its possession is not as serious as having other drugs. Most jurisdictions now treat hallucinogenics, such as LSD (lysergic acid and related compounds), the same as

narcotic drugs under the law. The same is true of meth-
adrine ("speed").

State Laws

Most states have laws prohibiting the manufacture, sale,
purchase, possession, or dispensation of narcotic drugs.

> *Examples*
> 1. Paul, 23-years-old, offers Louise, a high-
>   school student, a marijuana cigarette. She
>   accepts it. Both Paul and Louise have vio-
>   lated the law, although Paul would probably
>   be subjected to the greater penalty. As a
>   practical matter, Louise would probably not
>   be prosecuted if she agreed to testify against
>   Paul.
> 2. Joe sells heroin to Tom, Dick, and Harry,
>   who in turn sell it to other persons at twice
>   the price they paid for it. Joe, the whole-
>   saler, and Tom, Dick and Harry, the retail-
>   ers, have all violated the law. Again, since
>   Joe is the most serious offender, the prosecu-
>   tion would probably treat the retailers more
>   leniently if they cooperated in prosecuting
>   Joe.
> 3. Jim and Frank, highschool students, manu-
>   facture LSD in the high school chemistry
>   lab and distribute the drug to other stu-
>   dents. In many states all of the students
>   would have violated the law.

Federal Laws

Congress has made it "unlawful to import or bring any
narcotic drug into the United States," and "whoever . . .
receives, conceals, buys, sells, or in any manner facilitates

the transportation, concealment, or sale of any such narcotic drug after being brought in, knowing the same to have been imported or brought into the United States contrary to law, or conspires to commit any of such acts" also commits a federal offense. The penalty is five to twenty years imprisonment and, in addition, a fine of not more than $20,000. A subsequent offense calls for ten to forty years imprisonment in addition to the fine.

In order to make a federal case for sale of narcotics, the government must prove three elements of the offense: (1) that the defendant sold the narcotic drugs; (2) that the narcotic drugs had been imported contrary to law; and (3) that the defendant knew the narcotic drugs had been imported unlawfully. Although the evidence alone may be adequate in many cases to sustain a state conviction, in order to justify a federal conviction the additional elements of unlawful import and knowledge of unlawful import must be proved.

Other federal narcotics offenses are the carrying of narcotics on a vessel of the United States while engaged on a foreign voyage and the use of a communications facility (e.g., a telephone) in an unlawful narcotics transaction.

Narcotic Control Provisions

Narcotic Drug Record Keeping

Both federal and state laws require that certain records be kept concerning the lawful possession, sale and dispensation of narcotic drugs. Failure to comply with such laws is an offense. Any fraud in the dispensation or use of narcotic drug prescriptions is also punishable.

Hypodermic Equipment

Unless a person belongs to an exempt occupation, his possession of a hypodermic syringe, hypodermic needle, or any similar instrument designed to inject narcotic drugs is unlawful. Usually exempt from this prohibition are physicians, dentists, chiropodists, veterinarians, nurses, embalmers, pharmacists, research scientists, laboratory technicians or hospital employees acting under the direction of a physician or dentist, and manufacturers of and dealers in hypodermic equipment for members of the exempt group.

Glue Sniffing

In many states, it is an offense to inhale the toxic vapors of any glue, cement, or adhesive containing specified chemical compounds, including acetone, benzene, alcohol, and ether. It is also an offense to sell those compounds to any person who the seller knows has the intention of unlawfully inhaling the toxic vapors.

Example

The parents of Sam, a highschool drop-out, have warned Dan, the proprietor of a hobby shop, that Sam is an addicted glue sniffer and that Dan should not sell him any glue. In spite of the warning, Dan sells Sam twelve tubes of airplane glue. Later, Sam is arrested while weaving up and down Main Street sniffing the fumes of the airplane glue. Dan is also arrested. Both Dan and Sam are guilty of a criminal offense in those states which have laws prohibiting glue sniffing.

Narcotics Sold by Prescription

If a narcotic drug is prescribed by a physician, dentist, chiropodist, or veterinarian, neither the dispenser (pharmacist) nor the user (patient), nor the person who has prescribed the drug, is in violation of the law.

CAMPBELL HIGH
SCHOOL LIBRARY

Example

Tom has an impacted wisdom tooth. His dentist has prescribed codeine to relieve the pain. Tom takes the prescription to the local drug store, where the pharmacist fills it. Tom, his dentist, and the pharmacist all have acted within the law. If Tom were in a hospital and the codeine were administered by a nurse according to a physician's instructions, she too would have acted lawfully.

Narcotics Addiction

The Supreme Court of the United States has held that since narcotic addiction is an illness an addict cannot be criminally prosecuted for being an addict. To do so, said the Court, is a violation of the constitutional prohibition against "cruel and unusual punishment." The Court's ruling does not mean, though, that an addict is immune from the law prohibiting *possession* of narcotics. Nor does it mean that an addict is immune from punishment for offenses he may commit in order to support his addiction.

Examples

1. Bill and Bob are arrested while "high" on heroin. Both admit they are addicts. A tinfoil packet containing narcotics is found on Bob's person. No drugs are found on Bill. Bill is guilty of no offense. Bob has violated the law because he possessed narcotics, not because he was addicted to or under the influence of them.
2. Jack, a narcotics addict, is caught in the commission of a burglary. At his trial, he contends that his addiction compelled him to steal in order to secure the money needed to buy narcotics. His defense is invalid.

DEADLY WEAPONS

The possession, use and sale of dangerous weapons have
long been the concern of law enforcement. Most laws
relating to deadly weapons are based upon the rationale
that the possession, use and sale of weapons inherently
dangerous to human life constitute a sufficient hazard to
society to call for prohibition. Most state legislatures have
also decided that even weapons which are not inherently
dangerous to human life constitute a hazard to society
when misused and that they warrant appropriate restrictive legislation.

Prohibited Deadly Weapons

The sale, purchase, manufacture, or possession of certain weapons is absolutely prohibited in many states.
Included in this category of weapons are the machine gun,
bludgeon, blackjack, slingshot, sand club, sandbag, sawed-
off shotgun, metal knuckles, switch blade knife, bomb,
grenade, and Molotov coktail.

Unlawful Intent

The possession of weapons of another category constitutes a criminal violation only if the possession is with an
intent to use the weapon unlawfully. The unlawful intent
is usually inferred from the circumstances under which
the weapons are possessed. Included in this category are
the dagger, dirk, billy club, knife, razor and stiletto.

Prohibited Offensive Weapons

The possession or use of tear gas projectors, stink bombs,
spring guns, and silencers for firearms is either prohibited
outright or strictly regulated in most jurisdictions.

Concealed Firearms

Although the Second Amendment to the United States
Constitution speaks of "the right of the people to keep and

bear arms," the courts have stated that the provision does not prohibit the federal or state governments from enacting reasonable regulations on the use and possession of firearms. In all states, it is an offense for an individual to carry a pistol or other hand gun concealed on or about his person. In some jurisdictions, it is an offense to carry any kind of firearm, regardless of size, concealed on the person. Some states also make it an offense to carry a concealed hand gun or firearm in an automobile.

The courts have held that when any part of the weapon is visible to the eye it is not "concealed," within the meaning of the law. In some states, it is no offense to carry a "concealed weapon" if the firearm is "not immediately accessible" to that person, which means not within easy reach or under the control of its possessor.

Examples

1. Bob, a cowboy, visited a big Eastern city for the first time. Having heard the President speak about "crime in the streets" in the big cities, Bob carried his six-shooters in a double holster on the outside of his coat. While strolling down the main street, Bob was arrested and charged with carrying a concealed weapon. The charge was invalid. The firearms were not concealed; they were in open view. If Bob's conduct were frightening or disturbing to the people who observed him, he could be charged with "disorderly conduct," but not with violating a weapon law.

2. Harvey was an avid member of a national pistol association. Exercising what he considered to be his "right to bear arms," as expounded in the association's bulletin, Harvey carried loaded pistols in the trunk

of his car, in the locked glove compartment and under the driver's seat. Has he violated the law against carrying concealed firearms in an automobile? The firearms in the trunk and in the locked glove compartment are not concealed firearms within the meaning of the law since they are not "immediately accessible." However, the pistol under the driver's seat is a concealed firearm because Harvey can easily reach under the seat to get it. The pistol is "immediately accessible."

Unlawful Sale and Purchase of Firearms

Some states have laws that prohibit the sale of firearms to, or the purchase of firearms by, certain categories of persons, including minors, ex-felons, individuals on probation or parole, mentally retarded persons, and narcotics addicts.

Exempt Groups

Certain occupational groups are usually exempted from most of the prohibitions dealing with deadly weapons. The most frequently exempted groups are police, jail or prison guards, military personnel, private watchmen, target shooters, hunters, and members of veterans' organizations.

Firearms Registration

Most jurisdictions have laws requiring a retailer of firearms to keep a register of all firearms sold or given away. It usually concerns the date of the sale or gift, the name, address, age and occupation of the person to whom the weapon is sold or given, the price of the weapon, the kind, description and serial number of the weapon, and the purpose for which it is purchased and obtained. Such a registration law permits law enforcement authorities to inspect a retailer's register and all his stock on hand. Some jurisdictions have recently enacted legislation requiring owners to register hand guns, or even all firearms. These laws provide a criminal penalty for the possession or ownership of an unregistered firearm.

At least one state has recently enacted a law requiring the licensing of all firearm owners. Ammunition may be purchased only after showing a firearm owner's identification card. The law provides a criminal penalty for ownership or possession of a firearm by an unlicensed owner.

In view of recent United States Supreme Court decisions, there is a possibility that some state firearms registration or licensing laws, if not carefully drafted, may be held unconstitutional on the ground that they compel a person to act to incriminate or to tend to incriminate himself. He may have stolen the gun or used it in a killing or in some other crime. Recent attempts to enact effective federal firearms registration or licensing have so far met with failure.

Defacing Identification Marks

Most states make it an offense to change, alter, remove, or obliterate the name of the maker, model, manufacturer's number or other marks of identification on a firearm. Often the possession of any such firearms is considered as presumptive evidence that the possessor has changed, altered, removed, or obliterated the identifying marks.

Offenses Committed with a Deadly Weapon

Most states invoke a stricter penalty for certain criminal offenses when a deadly weapon is used in the commission of that offense. The most frequent offenses that call for aggravated penalties if committed while armed are robbery, assault, battery, and kidnapping. At least one state takes an even stricter approach and creates a separate and distinct offense, with a mandatory two-year-minimum penitentiary sentence penalty, for the use of a "dangerous weapon" in the commission of the offenses of kidnapping, rape, deviate sexual assault, assault, battery, intimidation, grand larceny, burglary, resisting a police officer, and escape from prison.

ANNOYING AND DANGEROUS CONDUCT

Some offensive activities are too varied or too general to be outlawed in specific terms. For that reason, a few statutes or code provisions have been rather broadly worded. Examples are laws directed at "disorderly conduct" and "disturbing the peace."

Disorderly Conduct and Disturbing the Peace

These legislative provisions seek to prevent persons from knowingly committing acts in such an unreasonable manner as to alarm or disturb another person or persons. The gist of the offense is not so much that a person committed an offensive act, but that he knew, or should have known, that his action would tend to disturb, alarm, or provoke others. The emphasis lies in the unreasonableness of the conduct and its tendency to disturb. But what is "unreasonable" depends upon the facts of each case.

Some of the general classes of conduct traditionally considered to be disturbing or disorderly are: creation or maintenance of loud and raucous noises of all sorts; threats to damage property or to cause bodily harm; careless or reckless display of fireworks; fighting of all sorts.

Public Intoxication

A drunk weaving up and down a sidewalk is another example of annoying conduct that is usually punishable under laws declaring it an offense to be in a public place while intoxicated. Enforcement is generally reserved for the drunk whose conduct is of an annoying nature.

Although the Supreme Court has prohibited prosecutions for narcotics addiction, on the theory that such addiction is an illness, the Court has thus far refused to prohibit prosecutions of chronic alcoholics for public intoxication, holding that scientific evidence has not yet established that chronic alcoholism is an illness.

Mob Action, Unlawful Assembly, and Rioting

A group of persons acting together can commit an offense even though the conduct might not be criminal if performed by an individual. Such an offense is usually labeled "mob action," "unlawful assembly," or "rioting." The minimum size of the group required to make the conduct unlawful is from two to twenty persons, depending upon the particular state statute involved. Some unlawful mob action statutes contain a provision that permits any individual who is harmed to recover damages against the city, county, or state in which the unlawful mob action occurred, as well as against members of the mob personally.

The activities proscribed by the statutes include: the use of force or violence by a group of persons acting together and without authority of law which disturbs the public peace; the assembly of a group of persons to do an unlawful act; the assembly of a group of persons, without authority of law, for the purpose of doing violence to the person or the property of anyone supposed to have been guilty of a violation of the law; and the assembly of a group of persons, without authority of law, for the purpose of violently exercising correctional or regulative powers over any person.

Examples

1. The "boys" at Joe's tavern decided one evening to do something about the college students in town who were wearing their hair
long. The boys at Joe's all wore crew cuts
and felt that long hair was feminine and
Communist-inspired. The boys, all twenty
of them, marched onto the college campus
and proceeded to clip the hair, moustaches
and beards of all the students they encountered. Their conduct may be punishable as
mob action. The individual crime of battery
is also involved, of course.
2. The Jones family, members of a minority
group, moved into an all-white neighborhood. A gang of toughs stationed themselves
outside the Jones' home, vowing to rough up
Mr. Jones if he came out of the house. The
toughs are guilty of mob action.
3. To call attention to slum conditions in a particular area, a group of individuals banded
together and marched down the street with
flaming torches, threatening to burn down
the town if the slum conditions were not
remedied. They were guilty of rioting.

To protect the public from the results of riots, a few
states recently have enacted anti-looting laws. Looting
occurs when a person enters any building of another in
which normal security of property is not present because
of a hurricane, fire, act of God, or riot and attempts or
accomplishes a theft.

Example

A city was paralyzed by a severe blizzard.
As a result, neighborhood stores were not able

to open and the police were unable to patrol the streets. Joe and Bill observed a storm-broken window at the Big X Liquor Mart. They helped themselves to several bottles of liquor in the broken display window. In addition to committing the offense of theft, Joe and Bill are guilty of the related crime of looting.

Parades and Marching

A statute requiring a parade permit as a condition to conducting a parade or march, and leaving it to the discretion of the officials to issue or refuse to issue the permit, is constitutionally void as an infringement of the First Amendment freedoms of speech and assembly. However, parade permits with limited restrictions may be constitutionally acceptable.

Some of the permissible statutory restrictions on issuing a parade permit are: limitation of the number of paraders (although the limitation must relate to problems of pedestrian and vehicular traffic); reasonable notice to law enforcement officers of the organizers' names and the time and place of the parade; restriction of the parade to non-peak traffic periods, restriction of night-time parades in residential areas.

Restrictions on Residential Picketing

A few states have statutes which make it criminal to picket the residence of another person. Usually, however, no offense occurs if the residence is used as a place of business, if the residence is the place of employment when the person is involved in a labor dispute and is peacefully picketing, if the residence is a meeting place, or if the residence is commonly used to discuss subjects of general public interest.

BRIBERY

The offense of bribery occurs when an individual, with the intent to influence the performance of any act related to the employment or function of any public officer, public employee, or juror, promises or tenders to that person any property or personal advantage which he is not authorized by law to accept.

Example

John slips the clerk of a traffic court five dollars to destroy John's citation for drunken driving. John has committed bribery. (So has the clerk, as subsequently explained.)

In many jurisdictions, the offense is not negated merely because the person to whom the property or personal advantage is tendered does not in fact hold the position the offerer of the bribe assumes him to hold.

Example

Mike attends a coroner's inquest into the death of a pedestrian struck by Mike's car. Mike sees a man in a white coat outside the inquest room in the County Building. Thinking that the man is a deputy coroner, Mike hands him $500 and asks him to make certain that the verdict of the coroner's jury will be accidental death. The man in the white coat is in fact an employee of the County Building cafeteria, but he accepts the money without saying a word and happily returns to the cafeteria kitchen. Mike has nevertheless committed bribery.

The offense of bribery occurs even though the bribe is offered to an intermediary and not directly to a public official, employee, or juror.

Example
> Paul, a liquor distributor, is charged with the offense of gambling. George is a juror at Paul's trial. One morning during the course of the trial, Barbara, Paul's wife, meets Gail, George's wife, outside the courtroom and offers her several cases of champagne if she will convince her husband to vote for Paul's acquittal. Barbara has committed bribery.

The public official, employee, or juror who either accepts a bribe or solicits a bribe is also guilty of the offense of bribery.

Example
> Alderman Phil tells officers of the ABC Rug Company that if ABC provides free carpeting for his home he will vote for an ordinance pending before the city council to re-zone some residential property ABC owns which would permit it to build a modern rug warehouse. Phil is guilty of bribery.

A person who is not a public official, employee, or juror, but who does not inform the offerer that he does not hold any such position, also commits the offense of bribery, in some jurisdictions.

Example
> After leaving a building which he has just burglarized, Larry runs into Jim, whom he mistakes for a police officer. Larry says, "Officer, if you let me go, I'll give you this $50 bill." Jim accepts the money. In some states, his acceptance constitutes bribery.

The intermediary who accepts or solicits a bribe for a public official, employee, or juror, whether or not with that person's permission or knowledge, is guilty of the offense of bribery.

Example

In many jurisdictions, the cafeteria employee in our earlier example who was mistaken for a deputy coroner would be guilty of bribery.

If the juror's wife in our earlier example had accepted the offer of the champagne, she would have committed the crime of bribery even though she may not have communicated the offer to her husband.

CRIMINAL USURY

Under civil law, a person or business that charges more than the legal rate of interest for a loan (usually 7 percent per year) is in violation of the law. The civil consequences to the lender of a usurious loan, depending upon the particular state statute, are: the reduction of the amount of interest to the legal rate; the loss of right to recover the interest; the loss of both loan (principal) and interest; or the payment to the borrower of a penalty equal to an amount that is double or triple the usurious rate of interest.

In recent years, organized crime has gone into the so-called "juice" loan business, making usury a serious criminal problem. A juice loan is one in which the borrower agrees to satisfy the loan with monthly or weekly payments at an interest (juice) rate of a hundred, or more, percent per year of the principal. Thus, a borrower, during the course of a relatively short period of time, may have to make interest payments which add up to ten, twenty, or even a hundred times the amount borrowed. Borrowers who failed to keep up with the juice payments have been threatened, beaten, and even murdered.

In an effort to suppress the juice loan racket, several states have enacted stiff usury laws which provide a criminal penalty for the lender of loans who demands an interest rate considerably higher than the usury rate specified for civil purposes. The criminal usury rate is usually set at 20 percent or more per year.

Example

Mickey has incurred some gambling debts. He meets Tony at his local bar and borrows $500 from him at the rate of 10 percent interest per week. Mickey pays Tony $50 interest per week for several weeks without reducing the $500 principal. But he soon finds that he is unable to keep up the payments. He is not legally obligated to pay Tony the interest (juice) payments. In some jurisdictions, Tony would be penalized civilly, for example, by the loss of the principal. In many states, Tony would also be guilty of the offense of criminal usury.

The criminal usury law does not apply to licensed small loan companies which are regulated by other state laws.

Example

Ed finds himself indebted to several stores and companies. In order to pay off his debts and to have one monthly payment rather than more than twenty, Ed borrows $1000 from the Friendly Loan Company at an interest rate of 12 percent per month on the unpaid balance.

Ed soon gets tired of making his monthly payments and goes to the local Legal Aid Society for free legal advice, hoping to extricate himself from his obligations to the Friend-

ly Loan Company. In most states, Ed would
be unhappy with the legal advice. Although the
interest rate he pays may be in excess of both
civil and criminal usury rates, his state probably has special small-loan-company-licensing
legislation which authorizes the business activities of the Friendly Loan Company. Ed may
be comforted, though, by the knowledge that
at least he will not be beaten up or killed if he
fails to meet his obligations on the loan.

INCOME TAX EVASION

It is a federal crime to knowingly fail to file an income
tax return or to knowingly file a false or fraudulent return.
It is also a federal crime for any person to knowingly
assist or aid another person in preparing a false or fraudulent return.

Example

Joe is a *maître d'* at a fancy restaurant. He
receives a nominal salary from the restaurant,
but earns substantial tips from the customers.
Joe hires an accountant to assist him in preparing his income tax return. The accountant
advises Joe to report only one half of his gratu-
ities, on the theory that no one will ever know
the difference. Joe follows his accountant's
advice and files his return. Both men are guilty
of federal offenses.

Chapter 4

Interference with Law Enforcement and Judicial Processes

INTERFERENCE WITH POLICE

Many states have statutes which make it a crime to interfere with the duties of a police officer.

Example

Officer Jones observes Jerry, a bearded 16-year-old hippie peace-nik, throw a rock at marchers in an Armed Forces Day parade. When Officer Jones identifies himself and announces that Jerry is under arrest, Jerry runs away down a side street. Officer Jones gives chase, but is stopped by three of Jerry's friends, who deliberately block Officer Jones' path, causing him to lose Jerry in the crowd. Jerry's three friends are criminally liable for their conduct.

Similarly, it is a crime in many states for a person, upon command of a police officer and under reasonable circumstances, to refuse to aid in the apprehension of an individual or in the prevention of a crime.

Example

Officer Smith observes Edgar, a militant student organization leader, looting a Bar-B-Que

65

stand. Smith chases him. Edgar hurries to a
taxi stand and begins to enter a taxi. Smith
shouts his identity to the taxi driver and orders
him not to drive off with Edgar. Because he
is in sympathy with the student organization,
the driver disregards Smith's order and drives
off. Smith then jumps into another taxi and
orders its driver to follow the taxi carrying
Edgar. That driver is also a sympathizer of
the student organization, and he refuses to
comply. Both taxi drivers are criminally liable
for failing to aid Smith in the apprehension of
Edgar.

OBSTRUCTING SERVICE OF PROCESS

The obstruction of the authorized service or execution
of any civil or criminal court process or of any other court
order is a violation of the law.

Example
A deputy sheriff, in uniform, goes to the
high-rise apartment building where Reginald
lives in order to serve a divorce summons on
him. Lloyd, the doorman, not wishing to permit any annoyance to Reginald, refuses to permit the deputy sheriff to enter the building, on
the pretext that he is not wearing the clothing
required of guests in the building. Lloyd's
conduct is criminal.

TAMPERING WITH EVIDENCE

It is a crime for a person, with the intent to prevent
the apprehension of any person or to obstruct the prosecution or defense of any person, to destroy, alter, conceal,
disguise, or plant evidence, or to falsify evidence, or to
furnish false information.

Example

> Andy and Bob, strangers to each other, meet at Charlie's tavern and engage in a fist fight. Bob falls down and accidentally hits his head on a bar stool and dies. Andy flees the tavern. Charlie, the bartender-owner, in order to protect his good customer Andy, gives the police a false physical description of him. By so doing, Charlie has committed a crime.

PERJURY

Perjury is a false statement, made under oath, about an issue that is before a court, legislature, or executive branch of government.

Examples

1. Under oath, Walter testifies at a liquor license revocation proceeding on behalf of a tavern owner who allegedly permitted his premises to be used for selling liquor to minors. Walter states under oath that he was in the tavern at the time of the alleged sale and that it did not occur. It is later proved that the sale occurred, as charged, and that Walter was not in the tavern at the time. Walter committed perjury.

2. At a recess during a criminal trial for murder by shooting, Roy walked up to the judge and told him that the defendant was his brother-in-law and had admitted to him that he murdered the deceased. The prosecution informed the judge that Roy was unrelated to the defendant and had never talked to

the defendant, who was in continuous custody from the moment of the shooting. Roy did not commit perjury: his statements were not made under oath.

Perjury also occurs when a statement containing a major falsity is signed under oath or affirmation.

Example

An application for a driver's license in state X requires a statement of the applicant's age and must be signed under affirmation. No one in the state who is over 70 years of age is granted a license. Abner, 75 years of age, signs an application under affirmation, stating that he is 69. He has committed perjury.

If someone makes contradictory statements under oath at a trial, in many jurisdictions the prosecution need not specify which statement is false. If contradictory statements are made in the same continuous trial and the witness admits the falsity of one of his statements, he is not guilty of perjury.

Example

In a personal injury trial, Gordon testified for the plaintiff during direct examination that the defendant drove his auto through a red light before striking the plaintiff. On cross-examination, Gordon admitted that the light was green. Gordon would be guilty of perjury unless he admitted, during cross-examination, that his first statement was false.

SUBORNATION OF PERJURY

A person commits subornation of perjury when he induces another to commit perjury.

Example
> If, in the foregoing example, the plaintiff's
> attorney induced Gordon to testify falsely that
> the light was red (after he had first told the
> attorney that the light was green), the attor-
> ney would be guilty of the offense of suborna-
> tion of perjury.

PROHIBITED COMMUNICATIONS WITH JURORS AND WITNESSES

It is a crime in most jurisdictions for a person to communicate in a manner other than that authorized by law with
a person he believes to be a juror with the intent to influence the supposed juror in regard to any matter which may
be brought before him.

Example
> Nat is a neighbor of Carl, a juror in a case
> in which Dan, a friend of Nat's, is on trial for
> a criminal offense. During the course of the
> trial, Nat remarks to Carl one Sunday that it
> is a shame Dan is in trouble and that he has
> learned Dan was framed. Nat's conduct would
> be criminal in many jurisdictions.

In some jurisdictions, it is a crime to communicate with
a juror or a witness (or with a potential juror or witness)
in order to intentionally produce mental anguish or emo-
tional distress.

Examples
> 1. John is sitting on a jury in a case involving
>   an alleged assault on a company executive
>   by Bill, a union employee. As John leaves his
>   home each morning to go to court, several
>   of Bill's fellow workers shout obscenities at
>   John. Such conduct would be criminal in

some states. If the obscenities were vile
enough, other criminal laws might also be
violated.

2. Throughout the night before Will is to testify in a trial against Frank's brother, Frank
telephones Will periodically. Each time Will
answers the phone, Frank hangs up without
saying anything. By trial time the next
morning, Will is a nervous wreck from lack
of sleep. In some jurisdictions, Frank's action would violate a specific state statute.

It is a crime in most jurisdictions for a person to communicate threats, offers of reward, or false information to
any witness or potential witness with the intent to deter
the witness or potential witness from testifying freely,
fully and truthfully in any pending matter.

Examples
1. Andy, a member of a juvenile gang, the 10th
Street Toughs, is on trial for assaulting a
police officer. Bob, a neighborhood merchant, witnessed the crime from his place of
business and is scheduled to testify. Clyde
and Doug, fellow Toughs, go to Bob's store
and inform him that if he testifies at Andy's
trial his store windows will be broken. No
matter who Clyde and Doug say will break
the windows—the Toughs or some other
party—the two Toughs are in violation of
the criminal laws of many states.

2. Under the factual circumstances of the
foregoing case, Clyde and Doug advise Bob,
the neighborhood merchant, that they have
learned that he will soon receive a package
containing $1,000 on the condition that he

does not testify against Andy. Even though it is clear that the money is not coming from Clyde and Doug, the communication of the offer of reward is a criminal act, in and of itself, in many states.

3. Again, under similar factual circumstances, Clyde and Doug tell Bob that he must have been mistaken in his identification of Andy, since Andy was out of the city with them at the time of the crime. Although Clyde and Doug might testify to that effect at Andy's trial, the communication of such information to a potential witness with the intent of inhibiting his testimony is against the law in many states.

It is a crime in many states for a person to try to prevent the apprehension of, or to obstruct the prosecution or defense of, another person by concealing himself or by leaving the state to avoid testifying, or to induce a witness who has material knowledge to conceal himself or to leave the jurisdiction.

Examples
1. Tom and Candy are high school sweethearts. One evening in the heat of passion, while parked in front of Candy's home, Tom forcibly rapes her. Although Candy's parents report the crime to the police, they have second thoughts about prosecuting Tom. Prior to Tom's trial, Candy's parents take her temporarily to another state so that she will not have to testify against Tom, thereby assuring his acquittal. The conduct of Candy's parents is criminal.
2. If Candy voluntarily left the state, after her

parents pressed charges against Tom, because she did not wish to testify against him, she would be guilty of a crime.

3. If Tom's parents had offered to pay for a trip to Europe for Candy in exchange for her failure to report Tom's crime to the police, both Candy's and Tom's parents would have been guilty of "compounding a crime."

Chapter 5

Uncompleted Criminal Conduct and Criminal Combinations

A separate category of criminal offenses exists for conduct that falls short of a completed unlawful act. Such offenses are technically labeled "inchoate" offenses and fall within at least one of three groups: attempt, solicitation, and conspiracy.

ATTEMPT

A person commits the crime of attempt when he intends to commit a specific offense and performs an act which constitutes a substantial step toward its commission. "Mere preparation to commit a crime" does not constitute a "substantial step toward its commission." The courts hold that the difference between conduct which is a "substantial step" and that which is "mere preparation" is one of degree, and must be determined by the circumstances of each case.

Examples

    1. John, an employee of J. B. Smith, obtains some cyanide and puts it into a drink he serves Smith, to expedite an inheritance he

was anticipating. Smith becomes suspicious
and saves the drink for analysis by police
laboratory technicians. John is guilty of
attempted murder.

2. Bob flunked his medical board exam. Dis-
gruntled, he decided to go into the illegal
abortion business. He purchased surgical
equipment for that activity, but abandoned
the idea before making contact with any
prospective patients. Bob has not taken a
"substantial step" toward completing the
offense of abortion. His "mere preparation"
is not criminal.

In most jurisdictions, a misapprehension of the circumstances, making it impossible for the accused to commit
the crime he attempted, is not a defense against attempt.

Example
Tim fired a pistol at Hal, intending to kill
him. But someone, without Tim's knowledge,
had loaded the pistol with blanks. Because it
was impossible for Tim to kill Hal as a result
of someone else's action, Tim's offense of attempted murder is not negated.

SOLICITATION

A person, with intent to have an offense committed,
who commands, encourages, or requests another person to
commit that offense is guilty of the crime of solicitation.

Example
Mack gets into an argument with the bar-
tender at his local tavern and is ejected when

he becomes too boisterous. Furious at what has occurred, he offers a passing person $10 to throw a brick into the tavern window. Mack is guilty of the offense of solicitation (for criminal damage to property).

CONSPIRACY

Conspiracy is the agreement between two or more persons to commit a crime. Some states require that, in order for certain crimes to occur, at least one of the conspirators must commit an "overt act."

Example

Tom, Dick and Harry, local hoodlums, meet at Tom's house and agree that Dick will beat up Joe, who has been late with his "juice" loan payments. Tom phones Joe and tells him that his son has been struck by an automobile and is in the hospital. Dick then trails Joe as he leaves his home for the hospital, intending to assault him along the way. But before any harm can be done to Joe, Dick is picked up by the police. Tom, Dick and Harry have committed conspiracy.

In some jurisdictions, it would not have been necessary for Tom to phone Joe, or for Dick to trail him, in order to satisfy all the elements of conspiracy.

It is generally no defense against the crime of conspiracy that one or more of the conspirators are acquitted, prosecuted or convicted of a different offense, no longer in the jurisdiction, or lacking the mental capacity to commit an offense.

Example

In the foregoing case, if Dick had not been prosecuted, or, if he had been tried and acquitted, Tom and Harry still could have been tried for conspiracy.

Similarly, if Dick had been found to be mentally incompetent or had fled to another country, Tom and Harry still could be prosecuted for conspiracy.

In addition to the general conspiracy laws, there are in some jurisdictions, conspiracy statutes making unlawful specified conduct—for example, the federal violation of "conspiracy to cross state lines to incite to riot."

Chapter 6

Accessories to a Crime

Although there is no legal concept in the United States for "guilt by association," as such, under certain circumstances an individual may be criminally liable for the acts of another person.

ACCESSORY BEFORE THE FACT

Broadly stated, a person who aids or assists another person in the performance of a criminal act is regarded as an "accomplice" or as an "accessory before the fact." In most states, he is subject to the same penalty as the individual who performs the criminal act. One state deals with such conduct by means of the following statutory provision:

> "When one person engages in conduct which constitutes an offense, another person is criminally liable for such conduct when, acting with the mental culpability required for the commission thereof, he solicits, requests, commands, importunes, or intentionally aids such person to engage in such conduct."

Example

Abe, Dan and Fred agree to rob the City Bank. Abe drives Dan and Fred to the bank.

77

Dan and Fred, armed with pistols and wearing masks, enter the bank and hold it up. Abe, unarmed, waits in the getaway car. Dan and Fred are arrested with the loot as they leave the bank. Abe is picked up later. Abe argues that he did not enter the bank or rob, was unarmed, and never was in possession of any of the loot. Abe's argument is futile. He is as liable as Dan and Fred are for the offense of robbery.

An exception is made in the law covering accessories for a person who has a change of mind and who effectively terminates his own efforts in ample time, or gives a timely warning to the police, or otherwise makes an appropriate effort to prevent the commission of the offense.

Example

Rocky and Ben, syndicate hoodlums, receive a "contract" to murder Emil. Ben changes his mind hours before the murder is to take place and telephones a warning to Emil. He also alerts the police. In spite of Ben's warnings, Rocky successfully shoots and kills Emil. By his efforts to prevent the commission of Emil's murder, Ben terminates his liability for Rocky's criminal action.

ACCESSORY AFTER THE FACT

A person who, intending to prevent the apprehension of an offender, conceals his knowledge that an offense has been committed, or harbors, aids, or conceals the offender, is regarded by the law as an "accessory after the fact" and is criminally punishable. However, the penalty for accessory after the fact is usually less than that for the principal offender's crime.

Here is an illustration of legislation bearing upon such conduct:

"Every person not standing in the relation of husband, wife, parent, child, brother, or sister to the offender, who, with intent to prevent the apprehension of the offender . . . harbors, aids or conceals the offender, shall be fined not to exceed $1,000 or imprisoned in a penal institution other than the penitentiary not to exceed one year or in the penitentiary from one to two years, or both fined and imprisoned."

Example

John is wanted by the police as a suspect in the commission of a crime. He goes to the home of his friend, Hans, and tells Hans that he is wanted by the police and must hide. The police soon come to investigate, but Hans tells them at the door that John is not there, while John is hiding in a closet. Later, Hans drives John to the bus station and purchases a ticket to another city for John. Hans is criminally liable as an accessory after the fact.

Chapter 7
Minor Non-Criminal Infractions

ORDINANCE VIOLATIONS

Municipalities, counties and other state political subdivisions have legislation similar to state statutes, called "ordinances." They provide punishment for wrongful but non-criminal conduct. Vehicular parking regulations are normally governed by ordinances, but serious traffic violations, such as speeding and driving while intoxicated, are governed by state statutes. The penalty for violating an ordinance is usually only a fine. If a person cannot or will not pay the fine, he can be committed to jail to work off the fine at a set dollar amount per day.

A municipality or county does not have to prove an ordinance violation "beyond a reasonable doubt." Unlike charges for criminal offenses, charges for ordinance violations may be proved by a mere "preponderance of the evidence." Ordinance violation trials are usually termed "quasi-criminal" because they share characteristics of both criminal and civil trials.

CONTEMPT OF COURT

"Contempt of court" is the willful disobedience of a court ruling or regulation, or the willful performance of an act that is disrespectful to the court. Contempt can be either "direct" or "indirect." Direct contempt occurs in the presence of the judge, in which instance he has all the facts before him and can summarily punish the offender. Direct contempt occurs, for instance, if a person swears at a judge in open court during a judicial proceeding. In indirect contempt, all or part of the misconduct occurs when the judge is not present. A defendant who is charged with indirect contempt is entitled to a trial, at which the alleged misconduct must be proved. He even has the right to a jury trial. Indirect contempt occurs, for instance, if a person falsely announces outside of court that the judge received money as a bribe.

Contempt is either "criminal" or "civil," depending upon the nature of the penalty. If found guilty of criminal contempt, a person receives a set penalty. An individual who swears at the judge could receive a $100 fine or ten days in jail for his conduct. Most jurisdictions limit the penalty for criminal contempt to not more than six months in jail. Civil contempt occurs when a person willfully disobeys a court order. The judge may sentence him to jail (for an indefinite period) until he agrees to obey the order. If a judge orders a man to pay alimony to his divorced wife, and he refuses to do so, the judge may order him committed to jail until he agrees to pay. Likewise, a witness, not a suspect himself, who refuses to testify in court, or before a grand jury or a legislative committee, may be sent to jail until he complies with the court order, or until the end of the term of the court, grand jury, or legislative committee. The same is true for a suspect or an accused person who has been granted immunity from criminal prosecution. Thus protected from self-incrimination, he must testify.

Contempt of Congress is similar misconduct, but it occurs less frequently. A person is in contempt of Congress when he is willfully disrespectful during a session of Congress or during a committee hearing, or when he knowingly refuses to cooperate at a Congressional hearing, unless, of course, his refusal is based upon a claim to his constitutional protection against self-incrimination, in which event he may be granted immunity in return for his testimony.

Chapter 8

Mental Responsibility

A general principle of criminal law holds that a person cannot be held criminally responsible for an act unless the act was accompanied by an "evil-meaning" mind. In other words, a prohibited act is ordinarily not punishable unless performed with what is variously described as "criminal intent," "felonious intent," "malice aforethought," "fraudulent intent," "willfulness," "guilty knowledge," and so on. The restrictive principle, however, is confined to serious offenses. Certain other acts—the relatively minor ones— may be punishable even when the offender's mind is not "evil-meaning."

Examples
1. Larry, a customer leaving a restaurant, takes a coat off a coat rack, puts it on and walks off with it. It belongs to someone else, but Larry mistook it for his own and did not realize his mistake until the owner of the coat caught up with him several blocks away. Larry is not guilty of larceny or of any other criminal offense.
2. Max is stopped by a traffic officer for crossing an intersection without stopping. Max

said he did not see the stop sign. His failure
to see it is no defense.

In general, when the prohibited act is a relatively minor
one, and when the social need to discourage the particular
kind of conduct would be severely jeopardized by the
difficulty of proving the intent, then the courts permit
guilt to be established merely on the basis of the conduct
itself.

THE DEFENSE OF INFANCY

In earlier days the very young were not exempt from
punishment as criminals. A ten-year-old boy, for instance,
once was convicted and executed for killing his com-
panion; a child of eight who had burned down a barn was
executed. Under modern concepts, however, a person
under a certain age (13 years old in some states) is considered incapable of harboring an "evil-meaning" mind
and is therefore immune from criminal prosecution. Children under that age who commit prohibited acts are, of
course, subject to juvenile court proceedings, and they
may be placed in non-penal institutions for their own
welfare (with the expectation of rehabilitating them) and
for the protection of others.

THE DEFENSES OF COMPULSION AND NECESSITY

A person who is compelled by someone else to commit
a criminal act may invoke the defense of "compulsion,"
but not if it involves the taking of, or an attempt to take,
the life of an innocent person.

Example
A bank employee points a loaded revolver at
another employee and threatens to kill him
unless he makes a false ledger entry in order

to conceal an act of embezzlement committed
by the threatening party. Acting under such
compulsion does not constitute a crime.

"Necessity" is a similar defense. If a person desperately
needs to take or use someone else's personal property or
to intrude upon real property, his need constitutes a valid
defense against criminal prosecution. If a hunter is caught
in the mountains in a blizzard without food, he is not
guilty of burglary or larceny if he breaks into a cabin and
eats what he needs to keep alive. But the defense of
necessity is a life-or-death proposition. Consequently, a
modern day Robin Hood could not take a wealthy person's
money or goods and defend his actions by saying that he
and others needed the property more than the victim did.

The Defense of Intoxication

A person who is so intoxicated that he does not know
what he is doing is not criminally liable for an offense for
which "specific intent" is required. If the town drunk picks
up someone else's property and makes off with it, he may
successfully defend himself against a charge of larceny if
the court or jury decides that his intoxication was of such a
degree that he could not have intended to permanently
deprive the owner of his property. On the other hand, the
defense of intoxication cannot be invoked if the offense
involves only "general intent," or "recklessness." A motorist
who kills someone while driving recklessly because of his
intoxication cannot defend his negligent action by saying
that he did not know what he was doing.

The Defense of Insanity

According to a long established rule, a person is not
criminally responsible for an act committed while he was

"insane." The best known early test of insanity was that laid down in the famous M'Naghten case in 1843. In that case, the English House of Lords ruled that, although every person is presumed to be sane, no one could be held criminally responsible for an act if, at the time of its commission, and because of a "diseased mind," he did not know "right from wrong."

For many years the M'Naghten "right-wrong" test was the one that prevailed throughout the United States. Then it was supplemented by the "irresistible impulse" test: even if a person knew right from wrong, he could not be held criminally responsible if, because of a "diseased mind," he was unable to avoid doing wrong.

In recent years certain other tests have been tried. One that emanated from the Federal Circuit Court for the District of Columbia—the Durham test—was at first widely applauded, but only one other jurisdiction has adopted it and it has been rejected by other Federal Circuit Courts. It has since been considerably modified in its practical, case-by-case application. Essentially, the Durham rule stated that a person could not be held criminally responsible if the act he committed was "the product" of a mental disease or defect. But the most popular test today, and the one that is continually gaining in acceptance, is the so-called "A.L.I." test, a test formulated and proposed by the American Law Institute. It reads as follows:

> 1. A person is not responsible for criminal conduct if at the time of such conduct as a result of mental disease or defect he lacks substantial capacity either to appreciate the criminality of his conduct or conform his conduct to the requirements of law.
> 2. The terms "mental disease or defect" do not include an abnormality manifested only by repeated criminal or otherwise anti-social conduct.

A person who is found by any legal test for insanity to have been insane at the time of perpetration is always acquitted of the offense charged against him. If mental examinations conducted after his acquittal establish that he should be placed in a mental institution for care and treatment, however, he may be so committed in a civil proceeding.

MENTAL INCOMPETENCE

Regardless of an accused person's state of mind at the time of the act he is alleged to have committed, he cannot be brought to trial if his present mental condition is such that he is "unable to understand the nature and purpose of the proceedings against him, or to assist in his defense." In such situations, he would be committed to a mental institution and could be tried thereafter only if his mental condition were to improve sufficiently to satisfy the two requirements just quoted. In death penalty cases, there can be no execution if, prior to the time of the scheduled event, the sentenced person develops a mental condition that does not permit him "to understand the nature and purpose" of the death sentence.

Part II
LEGAL PROCESSES
FROM ARREST TO APPEAL

Chapter 9

Procedure between Arrest and Trial

Although the legal procedure followed in criminal cases is not uniform among the states, the differences in basic concepts and principles are slight. Similarly, there are few basic differences between the procedure used in the state courts and that of the federal system. The following outline* typifies the judicial procedure that prevails in the states and at the federal level.

By statutory provisions, an arrested person must be taken without unnecessary delay before the nearest judge or magistrate. What happens after presentation to the judge or magistrate depends upon whether the arrested person is accused of a felony or a misdemeanor. If the charge is a misdemeanor, the judge or magistrate proceeds with the trial, unless the accused demands a trial by jury or a continuance is requested or ordered for some reason. If the offense is a felony, the judge or magistrate before whom the accused is first brought conducts a preliminary hearing.

---

* Based on and adapted from the law school casebook, *Cases and Comments on Criminal Justice*, by Fred E. Inbau, James R. Thompson, and Claude R. Sowle, published by Foundation Press, Mineola, N.Y.

THE PRELIMINARY HEARING

This is a relatively informal proceeding to determine if there are reasonable grounds for believing that the accused committed the offense: that is under the circumstances, is the charge sufficiently supported to require the accused to stand trial? If, after the hearing, the judge or magistrate decides that the accusation is without probable cause, the accused is discharged, but that does not bar a grand jury indictment if subsequently developed evidence (or the same evidence) satisfies the grand jury that the accusation is well-founded.

If the judge or magistrate at the preliminary hearing decides that the accusation is a reasonable one, the accused is "bound over" to the grand jury: he is held in jail until the charge against him is presented for grand jury consideration, or, if the offense is bailable, the accused may be released after a bail bond is given, which insures his presence until the grand jury has acted.

THE HABEAS CORPUS WRIT

In the event an arrested person is not formally charged with an offense and is not taken before a judge or magistrate "without unnecessary delay," he, or someone on his behalf, may petition a judge for a writ of habeas corpus and thereby attempt a release, or at least compel the police to file a specific charge against him, in which event he may be released on bail.

THE CORONER'S INQUEST

Peculiar to homicide cases and conducted soon after a killing or unexplained death occurs, the coroner's inquest is an ancient proceeding whose function is to determine the cause of death. The verdict of the coroner's jury, which is composed, in some states, of six laymen selected by the coroner or by one of his deputies, is not binding on the prosecuting attorney, grand jury, or court. In effect, the inquest is merely an advisory finding which can be either accepted or completely ignored. Even though a coroner's jury may return a verdict of "accidental death," a grand jury, either on its own initiative or on evidence presented by the prosecutor, can find that death resulted from someone's criminal act, and then charge that person with the offense.

THE GRAND JURY

Many states require that a grand jury, usually composed of 23 citizen-voters, 16 of whom constitute a quorum, must consider the evidence against any person accused of a felony. In federal cases, too, the Constitution requires a grand jury to determine whether or not reasonable grounds exist for proceeding to a trial for the accused. The consideration of a felony charge by a grand jury is by no means a trial: only the state's evidence is presented; neither the accused person nor his lawyer is allowed to offer evidence, in most cases. The procedure is intended as a safeguard against a prosecuting attorney's arbitrary action, for without grand jury approval no felony case can go to trial.

The votes of 12 members of the grand jury are necessary to return an "indictment," also known as a "true bill," against the accused. An indictment must be obtained, in those jurisdictions in which it is a prerequisite to felony prosecutions, even though a preliminary hearing for the accused may have determined that probable cause existed for holding the accused for trial.

Unlike serious criminal acts, misdemeanors are usually prosecuted on a document called an "information," which is filed by the prosecuting attorney after he has received and considered the "sworn complaint" of the victim or of another person who has knowledge of the circumstances of the alleged crime. In some jurisdictions, prosecution may begin on the grounds of a sworn complaint alone.

THE ARRAIGNMENT AND PLEA

Following an indictment, the next step is the appearance of the accused before a judge who has the power to try felony cases. The indictment is read to the defendant or the essence of its contents is made known to him; in other words, he is advised of the criminal charges made against him. In many jurisdictions, he is given a copy of the indictment. If he pleads guilty, the judge can sentence him immediately. If he pleads not guilty, a date is then set for his trial. In some states, and in the federal system, the defendant may enter a plea of "nolo contendere," a plea which has the same effect as a plea of guilty, except that the admission cannot be used as evidence in any other action.

PRE-TRIAL MOTIONS

After the formal charge has been made against the accused, he may, in advance of trial, make a request to the court (file a motion) for certain court orders that can assist him in his defense or in the implementation of his constitutional rights. Here are some of the most frequently used motions.

Motion to Quash the Indictment. With this motion the defendant may question the legal sufficiency of the indictment. If the court decides that the indictment adequately charges a criminal offense, and that it was obtained in accordance with the prescribed legal procedures, the motion will be overruled; otherwise, the indictment will be

considered invalid and "quashed." Even after an indictment has been rejected and set aside, the prosecutor may
proceed to obtain another and proper indictment. The
prosecution is entitled to appeal from a court order quashing an indictment, since at this stage of the proceedings
the defendant has not been placed in jeopardy (i.e., his
actual guilt or innocence has not yet been under consideration); consequently, a subsequent indictment and trial
would not constitute a violation of his constitutional protection against "double jeopardy." The protection against
"double jeopardy" means that an individual is not required
to stand trial more than once for the same offense, whether
he was previously acquitted or not

Motion for a Change of Venue. A defendant may attempt to avoid trial before a particular judge or in the city,
county, or district where the crime occurred by seeking a
"change of venue." In instances in which it appears to be
necessary in order that the defendant may receive a fair
trial, the motion for a change of venue is granted.

Motion to Suppress Evidence. A defendant has the privilege of filing with the court, normally in advance of trial,
a "motion to suppress" evidence which he contends has
been obtained from him in an unconstitutional manner.
The evidence in question may be, on the one hand, a tan-
gible item such as a gun, narcotics, or stolen property or,
on the other hand, an intangible item such as a confession.
If the court is satisfied that the evidence has been illegally
obtained, it orders the evidence suppressed, which means
that it cannot be used at the trial. If the court decides that
the evidence was lawfully obtained, it is usable against the
defendant at the trial.

Chapter 10

The Trial

In all states, and in the federal system, the accused is entitled to "a speedy trial." The right to an early trial is guaranteed by the various constitutions, and the constitutional provisions are generally supplemented by legislative enactments particularizing and specifically limiting the pre-trial detention period. In Illinois, for instance, when a person is jailed on a criminal charge, he must be tried within 120 days, unless the delay has been requested by him or an additional length of time up to 60 days has been allowed by the court to the prosecution for the purpose of obtaining further evidence. If the accused is out on bail, he can demand a trial within 120 days, although in this instance too the court can allow the prosecution an additional 60 days. Unless an accused person is prosecuted within the specified period of time, he must be released; thereafter he is immune from prosecution for that offense.

An accused person is also constitutionally entitled to trial by jury, but he may waive his right to a jury trial and be tried by a judge alone. If the case is tried without a jury, the judge hears the evidence and decides himself whether the defendant is guilty or not guilty. If the trial is by jury, that body determines the facts and the judge serves more or less as an umpire or referee; it is his function to determine what testimony or evidence is legally "admissible," that is, to decide what should be heard and considered by the jury. The ultimate decision is made by the jury alone.

JURY SELECTION

In the selection of the jurors, usually 12 in number, the defendant's attorney as well as the prosecuting attorney are permitted to question a larger number who have been chosen for jury service from the list of registered voters. Each lawyer has a certain number of "peremptory challenges," which means that he can arbitrarily refuse to accept as jurors a certain number of those who appear as prospective jurors. If any prospective juror's answers to the questions of either attorney reveal a prejudice or bias which prevents him from being a fair and impartial juror, the judge, either on his own initiative or at the suggestion of either counsel, will dismiss that person from jury service. Although the desired result is not always achieved the purpose of the practice of permitting lawyers to question prospective jurors is to obtain twelve jurors who will be fair to both sides in the case.

OPENING STATEMENTS

After the jury is selected, both the prosecuting attorney and the defense lawyer are entitled to make "opening statements" in which each outlines what he intends to prove. The purpose is to acquaint the jurors with each side of the case so that it will be easier for them to follow the evidence as it is presented.

The Prosecutor's Evidence

After the opening statements, the prosecuting attorney presents the prosecution's testimony and evidence. He has the burden of proving the state's case "beyond a reasonable doubt." If, at the close of the prosecution's case, the judge is of the opinion that reasonable jurors could not conclude that the charge against the defendant has been proved, he will "direct a verdict" of acquittal. That ends the matter and the defendant goes free—forever immune from further prosecution for the crime, just the same as if a jury had heard all the evidence and found him "not guilty."

The Defendant's Evidence

If the court does not direct the jury to find the defendant not guilty, the defendant may present evidence in refutation. He himself may or may not testify, and if he chooses not to appear as a witness the prosecuting attorney is not permitted to comment on that fact to the jury. The basis for not obligating the defendant to speak in his own behalf is the constitutional privilege which protects a person from self incrimination.

The prosecution is given an opportunity to rebut the defendant's evidence, if any, and the presentation of testimony usually ends at that point. Then, once more, defense counsel tries to persuade the court to "direct a verdict" in favor of the defendant. If the court decides to let the case go to the jury, the prosecuting attorney and the defense counsel make their "closing arguments."

Closing Arguments

In their closing arguments, the prosecution and the defense review and analyze the evidence and attempt to persuade the jury to favor their respective positions.

THE COURT'S INSTRUCTIONS TO THE JURY

Following the closing arguments, the judge, in most jurisdictions, advises the jury members of the applicable legal principles which they should, to the best of their ability, apply to the facts of the case as they know them. The judge also presents the jury with written copies of his instructions and with certain written forms for the possible verdicts. The jury then retires to the jury room to deliberate the case.

THE VERDICT OF THE JURY

When the members of the jury have reached a decision, they advise the bailiff that they have arrived at a verdict and then return to the court room. The foreman, usually selected by the jurors themselves to serve as their leader and spokesman, announces the verdict of the jury. Insofar as jury participation is concerned, the case is then ended.

If the verdict is "not guilty," the defendant is free forever from any further prosecution for the crime for which he was tried. If found "guilty," in most types of cases and in most jurisdictions, it becomes the function of the trial judge to fix the sentence within the legislatively prescribed limitations.

In the event the jurors are unable to agree on a verdict—and agreement must be unanimous in most states—the jury, commonly referred to as a "hung jury," is discharged and a new trial date is set for a retrial of the case before another jury. Such a retrial is not a violation of the constitutional protection against "double jeopardy" because there has not yet been a determination of guilt or innocence.

THE MOTION FOR A NEW TRIAL

After a verdict of "guilty," the defendant is still provided with certain opportunities to obtain his freedom. He may file a "motion for a new trial" in which he alleges that certain "errors" were committed in the course of his trial; if the trial judge agrees, the conviction is set aside and the defendant may be tried again by a new jury and usually before a different judge. If the motion for a new trial is "overruled" or "denied," the judge proceeds to sentence the defendant.

THE SENTENCE

In cases tried without a jury, the judge, of course, determines the sentence to be imposed. In jury cases the practice varies among the states, with most of them following the practice of confining the jury function to a determination of guilt or innocence and permitting the judge to fix the penalty. For the crimes of murder and rape, however, most of the states place both responsibilities on the jury. The jury decides whether the penalty is to be death or imprisonment and, if the penalty is imprisonment, the number of years to be served.

In some states, statutory provisions prescribe that on conviction of a felony the defendant must be sentenced for a specified minimum-maximum term in the penitentiary—for example, 1 year to 10 years for burglary—and that the determination of the appropriate time of his release within that period is to be made by a "parole board," whose judgment in that respect is based upon the extent of the convict's rehabilitation, the security risk involved, and similar factors. In many states a judge is permitted to set a minimum-maximum period anywhere within the minimum-maximum term prescribed by the legislature. In other words, the sentence given for grand larceny may be 1 to 10 years, the statutory range, or 1 to 2, 9 to 10, or any other combination between 1 to 10. A minimum-maximum term means that the convicted person cannot be released before serving the minimum period, less "time off for good behavior," and that he cannot be kept in the penitentiary longer than the maximum period, less "time off for good behavior." In between the minimum-maximum period, the convict is eligible for "parole," a procedure yet to be described. When imprisonment is fixed at a specific number of years, the law usually provides that the convicted person must serve one third of the sentence before becoming eligible for parole.

Chapter 11

Probation and Parole

In certain types of cases, a judge is empowered by statute to grant "probation" to a convicted person, which means that instead of sending the defendant to the penitentiary the court permits him to remain at liberty, on certain conditions prescribed by law and by the judge. His background first must be investigated by a probation officer for the purpose of determining if he is the kind of person who may have "learned his lesson" by the mere fact of being caught and convicted, or if he could be rehabilitated better outside of prison than behind prison walls. In other words, would any useful purpose be served for him or for society by sending him to prison?

Among the conditions of a defendant's probation, the court may require him to make restitution of money stolen, or reparations to a person he injured physically. Some state statutes provide that, for a period of up to six months in misdemeanor cases, and up to five years in felony cases, a defendant on probation must be subjected to the supervision of a probation officer and, in general, must remain on "good behavior" during the period fixed by the court. Failure to abide by the conditions prescribed by the court subjects the defendant to a sentence in the same manner

102

and form as though he had been denied probation and sentenced immediately after his conviction for the offense.

A penitentiary sentence of a specified number of years does not necessarily mean that a convicted person remains in the penitentiary for that length of time. Under certain conditions and circumstances, he may be released earlier "on parole," which means a release under supervision until the expiration of his sentence or until the expiration of a period otherwise specified by law. A person sentenced "for life" is, in some states, eligible for release "on parole" at the end of twenty years, with a subsequent five-year period of parole supervision. Someone sentenced to a fixed number of years—for example, 14 years for murder—may be eligible for parole in some states after he has served one third that period of time. And a person who has been given an indeterminate minimum-maximum sentence, such as to 5 to 10 years for grand larceny, may be eligible for a parole after he has served the five-year minimum, less time off for "good behavior." A violation of the conditions of parole subjects the parolee to possible return to prison for the remainder of his sentence.

In order to encourage prisoners to behave properly, it is generally provided that they should be entitled to a reduction in sentence for "good behavior" while in jail. The formula for computing "time off" for "good behavior" varies among the states.

Chapter 12

Post-Conviction Remedies

After sentence has been pronounced, the defendant may appeal his conviction to a reviewing court, which examines all or part of the written record of what happened at the trial and considers the written and oral arguments of both the defense attorney and the prosecutor. It then renders a written decision, which either reverses or affirms the trial court's conviction and states the reasons for the decision. If the trial court's decision is "reversed and remanded," it means that the defendant's conviction is nullified, although he may be tried over again by another jury. A "reversed" decision ordinarily means that in addition to an improper trial there appears to be insufficient evidence upon which to try the defendant again, and consequently the prosecuting attorney may not make a second attempt to win a conviction.

A decision by the state's highest court affirming a conviction is, in nearly all instances, the final disposition of the case, and there is nothing else the convicted person can do but submit to the judgment of the trial court. But if the appeal involved a *federal* constitutional question or issue the defendant is entitled to seek a review of the state

104

appellate court decision by the Supreme Court of the United States. Such requests, known as petitions for a *writ of certiorari*, are rarely granted.

COLLATERAL ATTACKS

Besides the appeal itself, nearly all states in recent years have provided post-conviction remedies by means of which a defendant may attack his conviction. Such "collateral" remedies most often are known as proceedings in habeas corpus or post-conviction petitions.

Even after a conviction is upheld against a collateral attack in the state courts, if a federal constitutional question has at any time been presented, the convicted person has yet another remedy available to him—the *federal* writ of habeas corpus. In considering the petition for the writ, a federal judge has the power to return the case to the state court for a new trial or to release the defendant, depending upon the kind of error committed, and the evidence still available to the state. Any such ruling, however, may be appealed to a higher federal court.

PARDONS AND COMMUTATIONS

The Governor of a state has the legal authority to grant a "pardon" for any crime committed within the state against state law. A pardon, which may be granted either before or after sentence has been served, has the effect of removing the stigma of criminality. In some states, it restores the defendant's civil rights to vote or hold public office. The President of the United States also has the legal authority to grant pardons, but only for federal offenses.

An executive action similar to the pardon is the "commutation" of sentence. It has the effect of reducing or shortening the sentence rather than eliminating it, as in the case of a pardon. A Governor may change the death penalty to life imprisonment, for instance, or reduce a 25-year sentence to 10 years. Some states have a "pardon board" that conducts hearings and advises the governor to grant or to deny pardon or commutation.

Part III
CRIMINAL LAW
ADMINISTRATION

Chapter 13

Arrests by Police

An arrest may be defined generally as taking a person into custody for the purpose of charging him with having committed some kind of prohibited conduct. An arrest does not include questioning a witness to a crime. It does not cover stopping a motorist to check his driver's license or vehicle ownership registration, or to give him a traffic ticket. Only when custody occurs does a stopping become an arrest. Arrest, therefore, occurs only when a police officer shows his intention to take a person to a police station or before a magistrate or another judicial officer. The two forms of arrest are arrest without a warrant and arrest with a warrant.

ARREST WITHOUT A WARRANT

A police officer may make an arrest without a court order (warrant) when he has "probable cause" to believe a suspect has committed a crime. Some state statutes phrase the probable cause test in terms of an officer having "reasonable grounds," or "reasonable cause," to believe that the person in question has committed an offense, but such terms are just other ways of phrasing the probable cause test.

The probable cause requirement stems from the provision in the Fourth Amendment to the United States Constitution and from comparable state constitutional provisions protecting persons from "unreasonable seizures" and requiring that "no warrants shall issue, but upon probable cause." The two provisions have been read to mean that an arrest without a warrant must also be upon "probable cause," because, otherwise, it would be "unreasonable."

"Probable cause" does not mean actual knowledge: the officer need not have personally observed the commission of a crime. He need only have knowledge of facts and circumstances that would lead a reasonable man to conclude that the suspect in all probability has committed a crime.

Evidence Required for Probable Cause

The amount of proof necessary to satisfy the probable cause test is less than that required to prove in court that the suspect committed the crime. At the trial, the prosecution must present evidence to prove the accused person's guilt beyond a reasonable doubt. To make an arrest, however, a police officer needs only to show probable cause—that is, enough facts to cause him to believe, upon reasonable grounds, that the suspect has committed an offense. The following are illustrations of the fulfillment of the probable cause requirement:

> *Examples*
> 1. While cruising in his patrol car, officer Perry heard a female voice from an alley, yelling, "Help! Thief!" Seconds later he observed

Jerry running down an alley away from the source of the shouts for help. Perry chased Jerry and apprehended him. Perry had probable cause to arrest Jerry, even though subsequent events established that Jerry was not the thief.

2. Cruising in a patrol car at three a.m. in a neighborhood that had recently experienced a number of burglaries, Officer Leonard observed Marty walking down an alley carrying a portable TV set, a small leather case, and several other objects. When Marty saw the police car, he dropped the items he was carrying and started to run away. Leonard had probable cause to arrest him.

Mere suspicion or a "hunch," however, does not justify an arrest.

Example

Julius, known by the police to be a dope peddler, was seen by Officer Howard walking hastily to get into a cab. The officer arrested and searched him for narcotics. Howard's action was not based upon probable cause, and the arrest and search were illegal.

Hearsay Evidence and Informer's Tips

Under most circumstances, "hearsay evidence," which may be described loosely as secondhand evidence, cannot be used at the trial of an accused person. Most often, it is information received by the police from an informer, and as such it may be used to establish probable cause for an arrest if it can be corroborated in some way. Confirmation of hearsay evidence is possible in either of two ways:

(a) If a police officer observes certain suspicious activities or has knowledge of pertinent facts or circumstances which substantiate the tip given by an informer, probable cause exists for an arrest.

Example
Steve told Officer Potts that Marvin was selling policy tickets on a street corner. Officer Potts, in an unmarked parked car, later saw Marvin conduct suspicious transactions with about 20 people in the course of half an hour. Each person gave Marvin something in return for something else. Although Officer Potts could not tell exactly what was exchanged, his observations, coupled with the informer's tip, gave him probable cause to arrest Marvin.

(b) If a police officer has contact with an informer who has previously given him consistently reliable tips, he may rely upon that informer's information to make an arrest:

Example
Leroy told Officer Roberts that he saw Hank selling narcotics. Leroy described Hank and said where he would be that night for the purpose of making his sales. Upon several prior occasions, whenever Leroy gave Officer Roberts such information, Roberts always found narcotics on the person "fingered" by Leroy. Under the circumstances, Roberts would have probable cause to arrest Hank.

Of interest in connection with hearsay evidence situations is the fact that, when an informer has furnished such information, his identity does not have to be disclosed at the defendant's trial *unless* the informer participated in the transaction, the informer was a witness to the particular crime for which the arrest was made, or the informer was present at the time of arrest.

Consequences of an Invalid Arrest

There are several consequences of an invalid arrest by a police officer:

1. Any evidence that is obtained as a result of an invalid arrest will be suppressed and excluded at the trial. The theory behind this "exclusionary rule" is that it will discourage illegal police actions.

2. Any invalid arrest can also result in a successful false arrest action against the arresting officer; a successful federal civil rights action against the arresting officer in the federal court; and (a remedy to be subsequently discussed) departmental disciplinary action.

An invalid arrest by itself, however, will not result in the acquittal of an accused person whose guilt can be proved beyond a reasonable doubt by other, independent evidence—that is, by evidence "untainted" by the invalid arrest.

ARREST WITH A WARRANT

The legal requirements for an arrest made with a court warrant are the same as those for an arrest without a warrant. Both must be based upon probable cause. A warrant for an arrest may be obtained by presenting to a judge or magistrate a "complaint" (charge), made under oath, which contains statements that establish a probable cause to believe that the person named in the warrant committed the crime described. The same kind of evidence that may establish probable cause for an arrest without a warrant (e.g., hearsay bolstered by other factors, as previously illustrated) may also justify the issuance of a warrant by a judge or magistrate. The following example demonstrates probable cause for the issuance of an arrest warrant:

> Chuck is a hotel keeper. Joe tells him that Sadie performs acts of prostitution in her hotel room. Joe says that he too had engaged Sadie's services. On several occasions, Chuck sees six men enter and leave Sadie's room at intervals of about a half hour. Such information, submitted by Chuck under oath, would justify an arrest warrant.

The following is an illustration of an absence of probable cause for issuing a warrant:

> Bill, a brother-in-law of Officer Mason, tells Mason that several persons have told him that Rose engages in prostitution in her hotel room. Without more information, Officer Mason's affidavit of what his brother-in-law told him would not justify an arrest warrant.

The following complaint is based solely on hearsay and does not show probable cause:

> Charles stated that Irving told him that Guy was a receiver of stolen property. Charles then stated in detail, without corroboration, the alleged illegal transactions of Guy as told to him by Irving.

In cases in which corroboration of an informant's tip is unavailable, the only recourse is to have the informant himself sign the complaint. That is seldom done, however, because the complaint and the warrant are public records, without the protection of anonymity. Most informants are not willing to risk disclosing their identities. Some jurisdictions permit an informant-complainant to use an alias in signing a complaint for an arresting warrant. But if he becomes a witness at the trial, he is required to disclose his real name. The arrest warrant must be signed by a judge or magistrate. Most state statutes also require that the judge or magistrate first "examine" the complainant about the matters set forth in the complaint.

The Warrant Requirement

Even though time and circumstances may afford the police an opportunity to obtain an arrest warrant, an arrest may nevertheless be made without one whenever there exists probable cause to do so. In other words, although there are situations in which a warrant arrest may be considered advisable, there is no compelling legal necessity for a warrant when the requirement of probable cause can be otherwise established. Any officer who has reasonable grounds for believing that a warrant has been issued for a person can make a valid arrest of that person.

Example

Police Officers Al and Bob went to the home of Franklin for the purpose of arresting him. They had very reliable information about Franklin's activities for several days. Officer Al thought that Officer Bob had signed a complaint and secured an arrest warrant before arriving at Franklin's home. Bob thought the same thing. Neither officer had in fact procured the warrant. The arrest of Franklin is nevertheless proper because both Al and Bob had probable cause to arrest him without a warrant.

The Valid Warrant

An invalid arrest warrant voids an arrest. But not every irregularity in a warrant will invalidate it: the irregularity

must adversely affect the substantial rights of the suspect.
The following are examples of both inconsequential and
consequential irregularities:

1. The name of the person to be arrested was
   spelled correctly as "John Q. Smith" in six
   out of the seven places it appeared in the
   complaint and warrant. In one place it was
   incorrectly spelled as "John Q. Smythe."
   The warrant is valid.

2. The state arrest warrant statute requires
   that all complaints be "sworn to." Complainant Carl told Police Officer Jones about
   a crime committed by Sam. Jones prepared
   a complaint for Carl's signature. In the
   excitement, Jones neglected to make sure
   that the complaint was sworn to before executing the warrant of arrest. The judge who
   signed the warrant also failed to notice that
   the complaint was not under oath. After
   Sam was in custody, Jones presented the
   complaint to the judge and it was sworn to
   by Carl at that time. Such an irregularity
   affects Sam's substantial right to be arrested
   only on the basis of a warrant issued upon
   sworn complaint. Consequently, the arrest
   is invalid.

Consequences of an Invalid Arrest Warrant

Whenever the counsel for an arrested person seeks to
attack the validity of a warrant, he must file in court,
before trial, what is known as a "motion to quash" the
warrant of arrest. If he is successful—in other words, if
the motion is granted—the arrest will be declared illegal
and any evidence obtained as a result of the arrest will be

suppressed and cannot be used at the trial. In many instances, if the motion to quash is granted there will be no trial and the accused person will go free because, without the suppressed evidence, the prosecution would be unable to prove guilt "beyond a reasonable doubt."

Example

Pat was arrested for robbery-murder with a warrant based upon an unsworn complaint. When the officers searched Pat, they found a loaded pistol in his pocket. In this case, the pistol does not incriminate Pat as the robber-murderer, and so it could not be used as evidence either at the robbery-murder trial or at a trial for the crime of carrying a concealed weapon.

When a warrant is declared void because of a substantial defect, the arrest itself might still be valid, and the seized evidence admissible at a trial, if the circumstances under which the arrest was made would have justified an arrest even without a warrant.

Example

A warrant is obtained for the arrest of Tony on the charge of raping a child. Officer Parson looking for Tony near Tony's home, sees him pick up another child in his car and speed off. Officer Parson chases and ultimately arrests Tony. In his car, and within clear view of Officer Parson, there is a child's garment that is later identified as belonging to the raped child. On Tony's trousers there is a stain that is later determined to be blood of the same type as that of the raped victim.

Even though the arrest warrant may contain

a defect and be declared invalid, the garment
and the blood would be admissible as evidence
at the trial because, under the circumstances,
Officer Parson could have made a valid arrest
even without an arrest warrant.

ARREST BY A FEDERAL OFFICER

There is no single congressional statute regarding the
general powers of arrest by federal officers. The matter is
dealt with by separate statutes pertaining to particular
groups of officers. For instance, there is a separate provision for FBI agents which authorizes an arrest, without
warrant, for "any offense against the United States committed in their presence, or for any felony cognizable
under the laws of the United States if they have reasonable grounds to believe that the person to be arrested has
committed or is committing such felony." Another statute
confers a similar power upon marshals and their deputies.
Still another prescribes similar powers of arrest for agents
of the Bureau of Narcotics. The various powers of arrest
by members of the Secret Service are also separately defined, as is true of other governmental units such as the
Bureau of Prisons.

LEGAL ALTERNATIVES TO ARREST

Most jurisdictions have alternatives other than arrest
for taking a suspect into custody to stand trial for a crime.
The alternatives are a "notice to appear" and a "summons."
They are most commonly used in traffic offenses. For example, the parking ticket instructing the owner of an automobile to appear in court on a specific date to answer
charges is a "notice to appear." The ticket given by an
officer to a motorist for a moving violation is a "summons"

requiring the motorist to appear in court on a specific date to answer the charge lodged against him. The consequence of ignoring a summons or a notice to appear is the issuance of a warrant for the arrest of the negligent person.

In recent years, the notice to appear and the summons have been used by some jurisdictions with increased frequency in non-traffic crimes. These procedures are especially effective for use in cases of minor crimes and in cases in which the suspect is a responsible member of the community and there is little or no expectation that he will flee from the jurisdiction before his trial date.

Chapter 14

Limitations on Arrest Powers

JURISDICTION OF POLICE ARREST

Unless there is a special law to the contrary, a police officer may arrest for probable cause only in the jurisdiction of his particular police department. Therefore, a state police officer may arrest for probable cause throughout the state. A city officer may arrest only in the city which his department serves, and a county police officer only in the county of his department. But a police officer who is outside of his own jurisdiction may effect a lawful arrest in his capacity as an ordinary citizen.

A police officer who observes a suspect commit a crime in his jurisdiction may chase that suspect into another jurisdiction and make the arrest in that jurisdiction. This is commonly called the doctrine of "fresh pursuit" or "hot pursuit."

Example

X and Y are adjoining municipalities. Pat is a police officer in X. While on patrol he sees Woody snatch a purse from a woman on a street in City X. Woody jumps into a car and drives away. Pat chases him on his motorcycle. Woody makes it to City Y, where Officer Pat curbs Woody's car and arrests him. The arrest

120

is valid even though Pat is not a police officer in City Y.

In many jurisdictions a warrant of arrest may be executed by any police officer of the state in which it was issued, but a police officer in one state may not execute an arrest warrant in another state. To apprehend an out-of-state suspect or fugitive, legal proceedings must be begun for his extradition from the other state. A federal arrest warrant, however, may be executed by a federal officer in any state.

FORCE PERMISSIBLE IN ARREST

A police officer may use such force as he reasonably believes to be necessary to make an arrest and to protect himself or another person from bodily harm while making the arrest. In most jurisdictions, however, a police officer may not use force which is likely to cause death or great bodily harm while making an arrest for a misdemeanor unless that degree of force is necessary to protect the police officer or another person from death or great bodily harm at the hands of the person to be arrested. The following is an illustration of the use of "excessive" police force in making an arrest:

> Officer Pat sees Jeff, a juvenile, steal several quarters from a newsstand and ride away on his motorbike. Pat is on foot. Pat fires his revolver at the fleeing boy. Officer Pat used excessive and illegal force in seeking to apprehend Jeff.

POST-ARREST POLICE OBLIGATIONS

The laws of practically all jurisdictions require that when an arrest is made without a warrant the arrested person must be taken before the nearest judge or magistrate "without unnecessary delay." When the arrest is made with a warrant the arrested person must be taken before the judge who issued the warrant or, in his absence, before the nearest judge or magistrate in the same county.

"Unnecessary delay," as used in the various statutory provisions, is generally interpreted to mean a delay for any reason other than the unavailability of a judge or magistrate, or circumstances such as distance or lack of ready transportation. Some state courts give the phrase a more liberal interpretation by saying that it means only an "unreasonable" delay, and consequently the police are permitted to retain custody over an arrested person for a reasonable length of time; reasonableness is determined by all the surrounding circumstances of the particular case.

Examples

1. Burt is arrested by the police of City Y at 10 a.m. as he leaves the scene of a burglary. The police put him in a jail cell and keep him there until 10 a.m. the next morning, even though a judge was in a courthouse six blocks away. Such a delay is "unnecessary" and "unreasonable."

2. Five people see two men commit a robbery at 2 p.m. A witness to the crime, Willard, was shot in the foot as the result of an accidental discharge of a robber's gun. The police soon apprehend suspect Frank, who fits the description of one of the robbers, but they cannot locate Frank's brother, Bob, who fits the description of the other robber and who has a criminal record for robbery. The police delay taking Frank before a magistrate so that they can conduct a line-

up for identification purposes the next morning when Willard is expected to be released from the hospital. By that time, they also expect to have Bob in custody. A delay of that duration and for such purposes is "necessary" and "reasonable."

CITIZEN ARRESTS

For certain crimes and under certain conditions, a private citizen may make an arrest. The scope of his arrest power and the limitations upon it are usually specified in state statutes or in municipal or county ordinances. As a general rule, a private citizen may arrest for a serious offense, such as a felony, when it is committed in his presence. He may also arrest a person who has committed a felony elsewhere, other than in his presence. But he may not, in most states, arrest for minor offenses, particularly city or county ordinance violations, even when committed in his presence.

Illinois has one of the most liberal citizen-arrest authorizations. Its Criminal Code provides that a private citizen "may arrest another when he has reasonable grounds to believe that an offense other than an ordinance violation is being committed."

A private citizen, in making an authorized arrest, may use the same force as a police officer. But he usually may not use force which is likely to cause death or great bodily harm, even in the case of a felony, unless that degree of force is necessary to protect him or another person from death or great bodily harm at the hands of the person he is seeking to arrest. In a number of states, any male over 18 years of age is bound by law to assist a police officer in making an arrest if he is commanded to do so.

Chapter 15

Stop-and-Frisk

Although the police practice of stopping and frisking people under circumstances reasonably indicative of criminality is a long standing one, the constitutional authorization for and the legal limitations upon the practice were shrouded with uncertainty until the 1968 United States Supreme Court decision in the case of *Terry v. Ohio.* The decision did not dispel all of the uncertainty, but it did sanction the stop-and-frisk practice in general, and in it the Court attempted to lay down some understandable rules for police to follow.

LEGAL GUIDELINES AND LIMITATIONS

In *Terry v. Ohio,* the Court held that when a police officer

    (1) "observes unusual conduct which leads him reasonably to conclude in light of his experience that criminality may be afoot and that the persons with whom he is dealing may be armed and presently dangerous," and when

    (2) "in the course of investigating this be-

havior he identifies himself as a policeman and makes reasonable inquiries," and
when

(3) "nothing in the initial stages of the encounter serves to dispel his reasonable fear
for his own or others' safety,"

then the officer "is entitled for the protection of himself
and others in the area to conduct a carefully limited search
of the outer clothing of such persons in an attempt to discover weapons which might be used to assault him."

As is readily apparent, the Court's language strictly
limits the circumstances that justify the "stop" and the
scope of the "frisk." Unless all of the prerequisites spelled
out by the Court are met, an investigating officer's conduct
may lack legal validity, and, among other possible consequences, a seized weapon could be suppressed as evidence.
The following are case situations illustrating proper as well
as improper stop-and-frisk practices:

1. Tom, Dick and Harry were seen by Officer
Jones standing and talking on a street corner. All three men took turns walking to a
jewelry store half-way down the block. One
man would look into the store and report
back to the other two. One man kept his
right hand in his overcoat pocket most of the
time. Officer Jones approached the men,
identified himself, and asked their names
and the reason for being in the area. They
said nothing (or else they gave an implau-
sible explanation). Jones frisked them and
recovered a revolver from the overcoat
pocket of one of them. Jones' stop-and-frisk
of the three suspects was proper, and the
evidence seized is usable in court.

2. For several hours, Officer Smith watched Sam standing in front of a restaurant. During that time, Sam spoke with eight known addicts. He entered the restaurant and spoke with three more addicts. Officer Smith entered the restaurant, identified himself, told Sam to come outside and said, "You know what I am after." Sam mumbled an inaudible response and Smith reached into Sam's pocket and pulled out several glassine envelopes of Heroin. Smith's action was improper because he acted not for his own protection and because he reached into Sam's pocket without first "patting him down."

3. Millie was a beauty contestant from Turkey in the Miss World Contest held in Des Moines, Iowa. Officer Sherlock posed as a judge in the beauty contest in order to gather information about narcotics that were being smuggled into Des Moines from the Middle East. In order to get a date with Millie, Sherlock led her to believe he would vote for her. They parked in Sherlock's car. He noticed a strange bulge in Millie's clothing. Thinking it was a Mid-Eastern Sabre, he proceeded to "pat her down." Wishing not to offend the contest judge, Millie let Sherlock continue until she discovered that in the process he had recovered the sabre and Heroin as well. Sherlock's conduct was improper. He was required to identify himself as a police officer.

4. There were several strong-arm robberies by

juveniles in the 19th Police District. On Saturday night, Captain Tracy saturated the district with officers and set up a "dragnet." During the evening, 100 youths were stopped and frisked. Such police action was improper because there were no reasonable grounds to believe that any particular youth was involved in criminal activity.

Although the right of a police officer to conduct a stop-and-frisk search is not conditioned upon legislative authorization, several states have enacted stop-and-frisk statutes and more are contemplated.

FORCE PERMISSIBLE

An officer may use reasonable, minimal force in executing a stop-and-frisk search. He may never use force that is likely to cause death or serious bodily harm. (For the legal limitations upon police questioning of suspects in stop-and-frisk searches, see Chapter 17.)

Example

While Officers Bob and Bill were making a stop-and-frisk search of two juvenile robbery suspects in front of a pool hall, the two youths started to run away. Bob and Bill chased the youths, caught and tackled them. Such police conduct was proper, but it would have been improper for the officers to fire their revolvers at the fleeing suspects.

Chapter 16

Search and Seizure by Police

In addition to having the authority to make arrests, the police are authorized to search for, and to seize, evidence of guilt on or about any person who has been arrested. In order to protect himself and other people against hidden weapons, a police officer making an arrest may also search for, and seize, any weapons possessed by or within easy access of the arrested person. Various limitations have been placed upon the police power of search and seizure, and certain penalties have been provided for the purpose of getting police compliance. Civil suits or criminal actions may be initiated against police who violate the prescribed rules. Another remedy, one which was developed by the courts without any impetus from the legislatures is the previously mentioned rule which prohibits using at a trial any evidence of guilt obtained as a result of a violation of the laws and limitations governing search and seizure. The underlying theory behind this exclusionary rule is the discouragement of police misconduct by putting the police on notice that they will be unable to make any legal use of what they obtain illegally.

Since the Supreme Court of the United States held in the 1961 case of *Mapp v. Ohio* that the exclusionary rule is constitutionally required (in implementation of the

Fourth Amendment's protection against unreasonable search and seizure), all courts, state as well as federal, are prohibited from accepting illegally seized evidence.

SEARCH WITHOUT A WARRANT

After a lawful arrest has been made, a police officer may search an arrested person and the immediate surroundings. Some of the purposes which justify such a search are the following:

(a) A police officer may search an arrested person for the purpose of protecting himself or others against attack.

Example

> Officer Jones makes a lawful arrest of robbery suspect Clyde in his automobile. Jones may search for weapons on the seat of the car and on Clyde himself, for the protection of Jones's own safety.

(b) A police officer may search an arrested person for the purpose of preventing escape.

Example

> Officer Smith arrests Joe at the scene of a burglary. Before putting Joe in the police car, Smith may search him for any weapon or instrument which might be used by Joe in attempting to escape from custody.

(c) A police officer may search an arrested person for the purpose of discovering the fruits or evidence of the offense, or for any instruments, articles, or items used in the commission of the offense. An officer may also search for such items in the immediate vicinity of the arrest.

Examples

> 1. Officer Brown gives undercover agent Mort some marked money to purchase narcotics.

Mort enters a tavern while Brown remains outside. Mort gives Sam the marked money and receives a sealed packet in return. Mort turns the packet over to Brown outside the tavern. Brown field-tests the contents of the packet and decides that it is heroin. Brown enters the tavern and arrests Sam. Brown may search Sam to recover the marked money and other packets of heroin which may be on Sam's person. The marked money is the fruit of the crime, and the money and the packets of heroin constitute evidence of the sale of narcotics.

2. Bill is arrested in his rented room for the forcible rape and robbery of a young girl who later identifies him for the police as a part-time janitor at her apartment building. In most states (the ones with up-to-date statutory provisions for what objects may be seized as evidence), the arresting officer would be justified in searching Bill's nearby soiled laundry for blood or semen-stained underwear worn by Bill at the time of the offense, and such items could be used as evidence at his trial for forcible rape. In all jurisdictions, the officer would have authority to search Bill and the area within easy reach for any jewelry, money, or other possessions taken from the girl during the robbery.

(d) Although the police may search the person of an arrested individual and the immediately surrounding area from which he might obtain a weapon or gain physical possession of any object that could be used as evidence against him, the right to incidental search does not permit a search beyond that immediate area; for instance, if a suspect is arrested in one room of his apartment the police may not search the other rooms. Of course, a person who is arrested on the street may not be taken to his home or apartment in order for the police to make a search there incident to an arrest.

(e) The search of a person must have some relation to the purpose of the arrest, or must be for the officer's own safety.

Example

Officer White lawfully arrests Alex for jay-walking. White does not know Alex, and Alex's actions have not been otherwise suspicious. White searches Alex and finds a marijuana cigarette in his inside coat pocket. The search is improper and the evidence is not usable in court.

Time and Scope of Search

An arrest search must be made at the time of the arrest. A search of the area within the suspect's "immediate control" should also be made in his presence. An area within "immediate control" of a suspect, according to a recent United States Supreme Court decision, is the "area from which he might gain possession of a weapon or destructible evidence."

Example

Officer Art arrested Ben in Ben's apartment. Art took Ben into custody and brought him to the police station. Later that evening, Art returned to Ben's apartment and made a search. The search was improper. Either it should have been made in Ben's presence at the time of Ben's arrest and restricted to the area within Ben's immediate control, or else Officer Art should have secured a search warrant for the subsequent search.

The fact that a police officer has grounds and ample time to obtain an arrest or a search warrant does not make improper a search which can be justified as incident to a lawful, "on view" arrest without a warrant. In the rape case already discussed in this chapter in which a search was made for discarded soiled underwear, the suspect might argue that, since there was ample time to secure warrants for his arrest and search, the evidence was illegally obtained. However, even though there was time to secure such warrants, the officer nevertheless acted lawfully because he had probable cause for making the arrest.

Duration of Search

A lawful search may continue only until the purpose of the search has been satisfied.

Example

Undercover agent Arnold, using marked money, purchased narcotics from pusher Bates in the living room of his apartment. Thereafter, Bates was arrested by the police at his desk in the study of his apartment. A search of the top of the desk promptly led to the discovery of the marked money and more narcotics. After that discovery, the police continued to search through the drawers of the desk, and discovered some stolen property. The seizure of the money and narcotics was proper because the purpose of the search was to discover the fruits of the crime. The extended search that followed, however, was improper and for that reason the stolen property was unlawfully seized and therefore not usable as evidence.

Under some state statues, an automobile used in the commission of an offense, such as narcotics violation, may be seized by the police. Using such authority, a police officer may seize a car and any contraband in it after the lawful arrest of the driver or passenger, or after a non-arrest search has been made with a search warrant.

Force Permissible in Search

A police officer may use reasonable force and reasonable means to seize evidence during a search.

Examples
1. Police officers arrested suspect Jon for a narcotics violation. Upon seeing the officers, Jon attempted to swallow two narcotics capsules he was carrying. An officer grabbed Jon, shook him and forced him to cough up the capsules before he could swallow them. The police conduct was reasonable and proper.
2. Assume that in the above situation Jon actually swallowed the capsules. The police officers then took Jon to a hospital where, in spite of his protests, his stomach was pumped in order to retrieve the capsules before they dissolved. Such police conduct was unreasonable, and therefore the seized evidence would be suppressed.

The Defective Warrant

Even when an arrest warrant or a search warrant is defective (e.g., issued upon an unsworn complaint), if a search is made along with an arrest and for probable cause, the evidence obtained is usable at the trial.

SEARCH WITH AN ARREST WARRANT

A police officer who makes an arrest with an arrest warrant may make the same kind of searches that may be made along with a probable cause arrest without a warrant. In most states, the arresting officer does not have to be in possession of the warrant at the time of the arrest. It is sufficient if he knows that the warrant has been issued.

Example

Officer Abner has been instructed at the police department's roll call that an arrest warrant has been issued for Sid. While walking his beat, Abner sees Sid. He may arrest Sid on the basis of the warrant and may search Sid in order to protect himself, to prevent Sid's escape, and to discover any evidence or fruits of a crime or items used in its commission.

CONSENT SEARCH

A search may be made legal by the consent of the person to be affected by it or by someone authorized to act in his stead. A relative who lives with a suspect may consent to the search of the jointly inhabited premises because both parties have an equal right to the use and possession of the premises.

Example

Hal, a murder suspect, is in police custody. He tells police that the gun he used is in his home. When the police arrive at the house, Hal's wife consents to their entry and search

for the gun, which they find. The search is
valid and the gun can be used as evidence
against Hal.

The rule permitting a consent search by a joint tenant
in order to bind a non-consenting joint tenant applies even
though the co-tenants are not husband and wife or otherwise related. In the absence of a familial relationship, the
existence of an equal right to usage and possession may be
inferred when the consenting person has a property right
or another connection with the premises, or with the
defendant, that signifies that he is entitled to bring guests
onto the premises. In other words, it must be adequately
shown that the consenting party has a right equal to that
of the non-consenting defendant to use and possess the
premises being searched.

Example

Ralph's girl friend, who occasionally spent
the night at his apartment, consents to the
search of Ralph's apartment while he is at a
tavern getting some beer. Ralph's girl friend's
consent is invalid. She did not have equal rights
in the apartment. Nor was she privileged to
invite or to bring friends there or to exercise
any other privileges that are normally those
of a co-resident.

Under most circumstances, a hotel keeper may not
validly consent to the search of a guest's or tenant's room.
Nor can a landlord give valid consent to search rented
premises.

PLAIN VIEW SEIZURES

Objects or materials which are not subject to lawful
possession—contraband, such as narcotic drugs—may be

seized if they are within "plain view" of a police officer in a place where he is lawfully entitled to be. A police officer is "lawfully entitled" to be in any public place, or, by invitation of a party with authority to invite him, in any private place.

Examples

1. Officer Burns observed Pete walking down the street. Pete threw away a package. Burns retrieved the package, which appeared to contain narcotics. The contents were field-tested and were found to be heroin. Pete was then arrested. The package was admissible as evidence at Pete's trial for the sale of heroin because the package was not taken by search and seizure, but was within the plain view of Officer Burns.

2. Officer O'Malley, equipped with a warrant to search Alfredo's summer home for gambling paraphernalia, saw in plain view a sawed-off shotgun in the home. Since its possession is unlawful, the gun could be seized.

SEARCH WARRANTS

Like an arrest with a warrant, a search may be authorized by a judge or magistrate by issuing a warrant authorizing the search of an automobile, home, office, or any other place. A search warrant may be executed without, at the same time, effecting an arrest. The search warrant is not conditional on any arrest. Indeed, there are times when the owner of a car or premises to be searched may be in custody already, or he may be many miles away. On some occasions, however, arrests are made at the time of, or following, a search that is conducted with a warrant.

Objects Subject to Seizure

At one time, in most states, the objects that could be seized via a search warrant were very limited—generally, they were limited to the instruments of a crime (e.g., a gun), or the fruits of the crime (the stolen property). Today, however, search warrant statutes of many states permit the seizure of additional items, including any instruments, articles, or things which may constitute evidence of an offense (for example, a blood- or semen-stained undergarment worn by a rapist); a human fetus (for example, in an abortion investigation); and a human corpse (for example, in a murder investigation).

Form of Complaint for a Search Warrant

A complaint for a search warrant must be signed under oath or affirmation by either a police officer or a private citizen. This person is called the "affiant" or "complainant." The complaint must state *facts* to show probable cause that the item to be seized will be found on the person or place described in the complaint. The complaint may be based in part on corroborated hearsay if there is "a substantial basis for crediting the hearsay."

Example

Officer Brown was told by Sid Green that a gambling operation was being run at Smith's barber shop. Green, who had given Brown reliable tips before, showed him a betting slip he said he obtained from Smith's barber shop. Brown surveyed the barber shop and saw a number of known gamblers come and go. Brown's complaint for a search warrant, based in part upon the corroborated information given to him by Green, was adequate for the issuance of a search warrant.

The facts to show probable cause may be obtained by an affiant who is an undercover, plainclothes police officer.

Example
Officer Green, in plain clothes, visited Joe's Cigar Store and asked where he could place a bet. He was invited to the rear of the cigar store where a wire room was operating. Green, although in disguise, was not a trespasser. Since he made no "affirmative misrepresentation" and had been invited to a place "open to the public," his complaint for a warrant was valid.

The complaint for a search warrant must particularly describe the place or persons to be searched and the things to be seized. The complaint (and the warrant based upon it) must leave the police officer who will execute it with no doubt regarding the place or person to search and specifically what to seize.

The premises where the search is to occur must be described in such detail that it excludes any other premises. The address, apartment number, apartment location, and any other descriptive data should be detailed. Usually a slight error in the address, however, will not invalidate an otherwise correct complaint.

Example
A complaint described a premises as apartment 2B in a three story red brick building with the address of 2300 South State Street. The description was correct but the address should have been 2310 instead of 2300. But there was only one building in the 2300 block

of South State Street, so the complaint was considered valid.

The complaint must describe in detail the objects to be seized. General and broad descriptions are inadequate, especially in obscenity cases.

Example

A complaint stated that at Edna's book store the owner kept "dirty, prurient, obscene and offensive books" underneath the counter. This description is inadequate. The complaint should state the titles of the books and contain other descriptive data such as author and type of book. If at all possible, a copy of the book should be attached to the complaint. (It should also be recalled from the earlier discussion on obscenity that special, speedy court procedures to determine the obscenity of books seized are also required.)

When a search warrant is for the search of a premises, the complaint does not have to identify the owner or the person in charge. Nor does it have to name the person in possession of the things to be seized, or any particular offender.

Form of the Search Warrant

Most of the descriptive data of the complaint (place to be searched and objects to be seized) must be repeated in the warrant. But a search warrant usually will not be quashed, nor the evidence suppressed, because of technical irregularities that do not affect the substantial rights of the accused.

Example

A warrant listed "Charles F. Smith" in three out of four places where the name was men-

tioned. In the fourth place, his name was inad-
vertently stated to be "Charlie Smith." The
warrant is, nevertheless, valid.

Any major defect, however, will render a warrant void and
result in the suppression of the evidence seized

Issuance and Execution

A reasonable delay between the date the items to be
seized are first observed and the date of the issuance
(signing by the judge or magistrate) of the search warrant
does not render the warrant void. However, the warrant
itself must be executed (served and the search made)
within a reasonable time after its issuance (usually within
three or four days). It may be executed either at night or
during the day.

The length of time during which the search is conducted does not affect the validity of the search warrant.
Nor is the validity of a warrant affected by an invalid
search that is made simultaneously with the search based
on the warrant.

Example

Police officers obtained a valid search warrant to search apartment 25 of the Jet Hotel.
They proceeded to the hotel and searched
apartment 25. But while in the hotel they also
searched apartment 26, for which they had no
warrant. The unlawful search of 26 does not
affect the validity of the search of 25.

Only necessary and reasonable force may be used to
gain entry into any building or other place to execute a
search warrant. While executing a search warrant, a police
officer may reasonably detain and search any person in

the place at that time, for the purpose of protecting himself from attack or preventing the disposal of the objects described in the warrant.

Warrants for Administrative Agency Searches

Health inspectors and representatives of other administrative agencies must secure search warrants whenever the occupant of a premises refuses to permit inspectors or entries.

COURTROOM CONSEQUENCES OF ILLEGAL SEARCH AND SEIZURE

As previously pointed out, if evidence is seized in an invalid search, the defendant may request the court (may file a motion) to suppress it. In most jurisdictions, such action must be taken before trial unless the defendant does not become aware of the illegal seizure until the time of trial.

In a few states, the prosecutor may appeal a pre-trial suppression order. This appeal does not constitute a violation of the defendant's protection against "double jeopardy" because jeopardy does not apply until the defendant is put on trial.

Chapter 17

Interrogations and Confessions

COERCION

Torture or any other form of physical abuse, or the threat of such treatment, might make an innocent person confess to a crime. For that reason, the courts have refused, for many years, to accept as evidence of guilt any confession obtained by force or threat of force. The courts exercised that power by invoking the constitutional guarantee that no person shall be deprived of his life, liberty, or property without due process of law.

A similar view has prevailed regarding confessions obtained after a promise had been made to a suspect or to an accused person that, if he confessed, the court would impose no punishment at all, or only a light sentence. The underlying theory behind that rule was that a person caught in a web of strong circumstantial evidence might readily confess if he were offered immunity or leniency, rather than continue to protest his innocence and risk a severe penalty, which in a murder case could mean death.

The general rule developed, and still prevails, that only a "voluntary" confession can be used in court as evidence of guilt.

142

Examples

1. The police suspected that Joe had committed a murder. They handcuffed him to a chair and started hitting him over the head with a large book or some other such object. They told him that the beating would continue until he confessed. Joe confessed. Joe's confession cannot be used as court evidence. The same result would prevail if it were the victim's relatives, rather than the police, who indulged in such conduct. The physical and mental effect would be the same and the risk of a false confession would be just as great.

2. Frank is told that, unless he confesses to the robbery-murder for which he is a suspect, he will be pushed out of a fifth floor window, or turned over to a lynch mob, or subjected to a physical beating by the police. Frank confesses. Frank's confession is not valid.

3. One evening, Pete got into a fight with Ed outside a tavern. Several hours later, Pete was seen leaving the rooming house where Ed lived. Shortly thereafter, a neighbor found Ed dead in his room. He had been stabbed to death. When Pete was questioned by the police, he readily admitted about the fight, but denied killing Ed. As for his being at Ed's rooming house, he stated that he went there to look for a former girl friend whose name he had forgotten and whom he was unable to locate. He also said that while in the rooming house hall, he encountered Ed, but that they only swore at

each other and that no physical encounter occurred. Pete's shirt had blood on it of the same blood type as Ed's, but Pete said it got there at the time of the tavern brawl. Pete was seen with a knife in his possesssion while in the tavern, but he had no knife in his possession when taken into police custody.

The police pointed out to Pete the implausibility of his story of innocence. They told him that a conviction for murder was a sure thing. They also told him that since Ed was a skid row bum and his death a good riddance, if Pete confessed they would recommend that only a charge of manslaughter be placed against him. They informed him that it might result in a one-year sentence and he would thereby avoid the risk of life imprisonment or death if found guilty of murder.

A confession obtained after such a promise of leniency would not be usable as evidence. It lacks the requirements of voluntariness, and, more particularly, trustworthiness.

Until recently, if any of the suspects in these examples had told the police interrogator where he had hidden the murder weapon or the victim's jewelry or other valuables, and if these items had been found at that location, both they and that portion of the confession thus substantiated could be used as evidence. The courts considered the element of trustworthiness as offsetting that of voluntariness because the voluntariness test had been developed only as a protection for the innocent. The theory was that a person who disclosed such details must have been telling the truth, even though the truth had been forced out of him. But the present judicial viewpoint is to outlaw such evidence in order to discourage the police from resorting to brutal interrogation practices.

POLICE DETENTION

In a democratic society, the police cannot have and are not given unlimited privileges regarding the length of time they may detain arrested persons, either for interrogation or for any other purpose. One requirement imposed upon the police is that the arrestee must be taken before a judicial magistrate or judge "without unnecessary delay." Although state courts have admitted, as evidence, confessions obtained during a period of unnecessary delay provided they were voluntary, the federal courts, for a number of years, have rejected confessions obtained by federal officers during a period of unnecessary delay and this was interpreted to mean promptly or immediately. This exclusion was applied without reference to the voluntariness or truthworthiness of the confession. The underlying court purpose was to force the police to comply with the requirement of an early presentation of an arrestee to the court. Recently, however, because of a dissatisfaction with its consequences of freeing many criminal offenders whose guilt was indisputable, Congress legislated this exclusionary rule out of existence. Congress had the authority, since the United States Supreme Court had not said that the rule was constitutionally required. When it originally established the rule, the Court had only invoked its "supervisory power" and said no *federal* court could use confessions obtained during a period of such delay. It had also held that the state courts were not obligated to follow this rule, since the use of such confessions, if voluntarily given, did not offend due process.

As matters now stand, therefore, in both federal and state courts, a confession obtained during a period of delay in getting an arrestee before a magistrate will not necessarily be rejected. However, the delay may be considered as a factor in the over-all determination of whether or not the confession was a voluntary one.

WARNINGS OF CONSTITUTIONAL RIGHTS

The Supreme Court of the United States, in the 1966 case of *Miranda v. Arizona,* held that the police must give the following warnings before they can interrogate a criminal suspect who is "in custody" or who "has been deprived of his freedom in any significant way":

(a) You have a right to remain silent and you need not answer any questions;
(b) If you do answer questions, your answers can be used as evidence against you;
(c) You have a right to consult with a lawyer before or during our questioning of you;
(d) If you cannot afford to hire a lawyer, one will be provided for you without cost.

The court decided that these warnings were required in order to accord to all persons the constitutional privilege against self-incrimination.

Under the Miranda decision, the only time the police can interrogate a suspect who is "in custody" or otherwise "deprived of his freedom in any significant way" is *after* he has been given the warnings and *after* he has expressly stated that he is willing to answer questions without a lawyer being present.

The Miranda rules have met with disapproval from many quarters, on the ground that they were not constitutionally required and that they have severely handicapped the police in their efforts to solve serious crimes. The Congress of the United States subscribed to this disapproval in June, 1968, by passing a statute aimed at nullifying the Miranda rules and substituting the original test of whether or not a confession was given voluntarily. Although the statute was necessarily directed only toward interrogations by federal officers and trials in federal courts (Congress having no such authority over state cases), if constitutionally sustained it ultimately will have a considerable impact on interrogations by state officers and on trials in state courts, too. However, until the Supreme Court acts in some future case, state and local police officers, and the courts of the various states, must continue to comply with the Miranda requirements.

Since the Miranda decision was based upon constitutional grounds, most legal authorities are of the opinion that the congressional effort to nullify it will be considered constitutionally impermissible. It is important to note, however, that the composition of the Court has changed from what it was at the time of the Miranda decision, which was handed down on a 5 to 4 vote. Whether change of justices will be a significant factor in any test of the federal statute before the Supreme Court remains to be seen.

As for what interrogation tactics and techniques the police may use *after* they have told an arrested person about his rights and privileges as prescribed in the Miranda warnings, and *after* the arrestee has waived his right to remain silent and his right to counsel, the only general rule is that the police must scrupulously avoid doing or saying anything that might make an innocent person confess to a crime. They may thus fulfill the basic requirement of voluntariness.

Chapter 18

Self-Incrimination

As discussed in the last chapter, police cannot compel a person to talk to them regarding an offense of which he is suspected or accused. Any confession obtained by compulsion, either physical or psychological, is void because of its involuntary and untrustworthy nature. Any evidence derived from an involuntary confession is not usable in court.

Legal controls also exist to restrain other forms of compulsion on the part of all governmental officials, governmental bodies, and the courts. The principal control stems from the constitutional privilege against self-incrimination, as stated in the Fifth Amendment to the Constitution of the United States. It is also available to suspected and accused persons at such governmental functions as coroner's inquests, legislative hearings and, of course, judicial proceedings.

HISTORY AND POLICY

The self-incrimination privilege, in contrast to the involuntary confession rule, was not created primarily for the protection of the innocent. It arose out of an early

148

practice in England in which persons suspected of heresy were brought into the church courts and ordered to answer to the charges made against them. A sufficient feeling of opposition to the practice gradually developed so that the church courts ultimately stopped it. Shortly thereafter, the law courts felt impelled to discard the practice of compelling testimony. In other words, no person accused of *any* offense should be compelled to incriminate himself.

In addition to the historical basis for the privilege against self-incrimination, there was another consideration for its acceptance and incorporation into our federal and state constitutions. There was a feeling that the police should be required to search for other and more reliable evidence than merely what a court or some other governmental unit could extract from the accused. The self-incrimination privilege, therefore, is largely founded upon a policy consideration—the sheer distaste for the idea that a person ought to be required to incriminate himself orally.

LIMITATIONS UPON PRIVILEGE

In view of the historical origin and the policy reasons in support of the self-incrimination privilege, what, if anything, can be obtained from an accused person, either without his consent or by actual compulsion? As a general rule, the self-incrimination privilege does not apply to anything of a *physical* nature that may have been obtained from an accused person.

To summarize, if the evidence sought from the accused is of a "physical" nature, it may be lawfully obtained "without consent" or "by the use of reasonable force and under reasonable circumstances."

There is another constitutional prohibition, however, that serves as a restriction upon the procurement of physical evidence by compulsion—the guarantee that no person shall be deprived of his life, liberty, or property without due process of law. It has been interpreted to mean that physical evidence of guilt can only be obtained by "reasonable force" and under "reasonable circumstances."

Examples

1. Phil, arrested for burglary, refuses to permit his fingerprints to be taken. His hands may be held in such a way as to permit the necessary procedure.

2. Moe and Bob are lawfully arrested for the possession of narcotics. Both put small plastic bags into their mouths. A police officer holds Moe's jaw and pulls out a bag. Bob swallows his. Bob is taken to a hospital where, over his protests, his stomach is pumped out and the bag is recovered.

   The narcotics evidence against Moe would be usable at his trial because the police action in removing it from his mouth was not unreasonable.

   The narcotics evidence against Bob, however, would be excluded because of the unreasonableness of the police conduct in having his stomach pumped. Such conduct has been described as "shocking to the conscience" of the courts, and thus violative of due process.

3. John Motorist is involved in an automobile accident. An investigating police officer suspects that he is intoxicated, so he takes Motorist to a hospital, where a physician is requested to extract, through a hypodermic needle, a sample of blood for the purpose of a chemical test for alcoholic intoxication.

> Motorist refuses to consent, but the blood sample is taken anyway, over his mild resistance. The evidence may be used against him.

The following are kinds of physical evidence that may be obtained without the consent of an arrestee, or by exercising "reasonable" force under "reasonable circumstances": "mug" photographs; fingerprints; fingernail scrapings; samples of hair; specimens of blood, urine, or breath; objects concealed in bodily cavities, even in the anus or vagina.

An arrestee may also be required to permit the removal of clothing to be searched for concealed items such as narcotics or jewelry; permit an inspection of his body for tattoo marks, scratches, etc.; try on articles of clothing (e.g., a hat left at scene of crime); appear in a police line-up for identification purposes; speak for purposes of voice identification by witnesses to an offense; provide specimens of his handwriting (e.g., in an extortion or kidnapping case).

Even when the evidence comes from the mouth, or through the voice, of the arrested person (or through some other act on his part), no violation of the self-incrimination privilege is involved, provided that it is to be used only for its physical characteristics and not for its value as "testimony." For instance, if an arrestee is ordered to utter the words "stick 'em up," so that a robbery victim can compare his voice with that of the robber, the evidence thus obtainable is considered to be of a physical nature only. The same is true of a specimen of handwriting that an arrestee may be ordered to furnish; it is solely for the purpose of a comparison between its physical characteristics and those of the document in question (e.g., a ransom note, or a forged check). On the other hand, of course, an arrestee cannot be compelled to furnish a specimen of his handwriting in the form of a statement of his whereabouts at the time of the crime. Similarly, with respect to photographs taken without consent, or over protest or resistance, they must not be in the form of a re-enactment of the crime to which the arrestee may have confessed, because in any such re-enactment his movements might convey his thoughts and, therefore, become the equivalent of verbal expressions.

Chapter 19

Police Encouragement
to Commit Crime

Out of consideration for the frailties of human nature, i.e., the cynical notion that "every man has his price," the courts have established the principle that, if the police "entice or induce" a person to commit a crime, he should not be punished for what he did. The feeling prevails that, except for police persuasion and temptation, the individual may have remained an honest, law-abiding citizen. Accordingly, the courts have provided him with the defense of "entrapment," which means, in effect, that he is granted immunity for what he did as a result of police encouragement. On the other hand, if the police merely afford a person an *opportunity* to commit a crime, he has no such defense.

Examples

1. Police Detective Healy suspects that Paul is a burglar, but he has never been able to "get the goods" on Paul. One day Healy, posing as an ex-con, has a conversation in a bar with Paul. Healy tells Paul that he can make an easy score at the home of Banker Adam, who is taking his wife to the opera that night. Healy tells Paul how to gain

153

easy access to the home. Then Healy ar-
ranges for a group of police officers to close
in just as Paul breaks into Banker Adam's
home. Paul cannot be convicted of burglary.
Police officer Healy "enticed and induced"
him to commit the act. The idea did not
originate with Paul. The defense of entrapment is valid.

2. Druggist Rex is suspected of selling narcotics unlawfully. The police arrange for a
known addict, Alex, to try to make a "buy"
from Rex. Alex is given marked money,
goes to Rex, and asks if he can buy a "fix"
of Heroin. Rex says he can let him have one
for $20. Rex hands the Heroin to Alex, and
Alex gives him the marked money. After
Alex gets out of the store and the substance
is verified to be Heroin, officers enter the
store, arrest Rex, and find the marked
money in the cash register. This is not entrapment. Rex was only given an *opportunity* to make the sale; he was not enticed
or induced to do so.

Chapter 20

False Eye-Witness Identification

As discussed earlier, evidence of a physical nature may be obtained from an arrestee without his consent or, under certain conditions, even over his objection. The same is true with respect to viewing the arrestee by the victims or witnesses to a crime; he cannot prevent the viewing by invoking the self-incrimination privilege. However, there is another constitutional right that is available to him in this situation—his right to counsel.

The Sixth Amendment to the Constitution of the United States provides that in "all criminal prosecutions, the accused shall enjoy the right . . . to have the assistance of counsel for his defense." This provision has been interpreted to mean that, in state as well as in federal criminal cases, any accused person is entitled to counsel not only at his trial but also at any "critical stage" of the investigation of the crime for which he is suspected.

The identification viewing process has been held by the Supreme Court to be a "critical stage." The underlying reason for the Court's conclusion is that, without an attorney to observe the eye-witness identification procedures used by the police, an unfair viewing may occur, perhaps even unrealized by the accused himself; and neither he nor his attorney would be able to disclose that fact or have it revealed at the trial.

Counsel's presence is considered a protection against a false identification from placing the suspect in a line-up with persons who are considerably unlike the description of the offender, as received by the police from witnesses to the crime. In such a situation, of course, the suspect would stand out prominently, which would amount to a strong suggestion that he must be the culprit and that an identification is in order. Another related concern is that perhaps the police, thoroughly confident of a suspect's guilt, might resort to various other forms of unfair suggestions and influences, and thereby induce an identification of the suspect could waive. The Court also said that is was not presence is looked upon as a safeguard against that possibility.

In the judicial decisions that laid down the accused's right to counsel at police line-ups, the United States Supreme Court said that the right was one which a suspect could waive. The Court also said that it was not foreclosing the police or the legislatures from establishing various line-up viewing procedures that would insure fairness to the suspect equivalent to, or better than, the protection that counsel's presence might afford. Perhaps a sound movie of the proceeding might be an acceptable alternative.

Before being placed in a line-up, a suspect should be told that a line-up is planned, that he has no legal right to refuse to participate, that he has a right to have an attorney present, and that if he cannot afford an attorney one will be provided for him free.

If a suspect states that he does not desire the presence of counsel, he may be asked to sign a waiver to that effect. If he states that he wants counsel, the line-up must be postponed until an attorney can be present. When counsel is present, he is entitled only to observe what occurs; he has no right to ask questions of the witnesses or to do anything other than observe. In all instances in which witnesses are to view a suspect in the station house, the suspect should be placed in a line-up with other persons of the same race and similar in all essential respects.

The consequences of a violation of any of the safeguards required by the Supreme Court may be the rejection of the identifying evidence obtained, either at the time of the viewing or when presented in the courtroom by a witness whose courtroom identification may have stemmed from what occurred at the station house line-up. In all probability, a line-up will not be considered necessary when the witness knows the suspect personally and has stated that the person he knows is the one who committed the offense, when the victim is in danger of death and may not survive long enough for a line-up viewing, or when the suspect asks that he be confronted immediately with the victim or other witnesses.

Part IV
The Citizen's Duty
and Protection

Chapter 21

The Citizen as Court Witness

It is quite common and natural for a person who, for the first time, is called as a witness in a criminal case to be apprehensive about testifying. The solemnity of the courtroom and the prevalence of certain myths that portray the ordeal of cross-examination contribute to this feeling of fear and anxiety. To lessen the apprehension, and to encourage effective testimony, we are presenting a number of basic rules of conduct for a citizen-witness in a criminal case.

1. *Tell the truth.* Never exaggerate or knowingly hide anything. A witness who is telling the truth as well as he can does not have to fear cross-examination by the opposing lawyer.

2. *Understand the question before answering.* A witness should never answer a question unless he is absolutely satisfied that he understands it. This advice is particularly pertinent regarding cross-examination.

If you do not understand a question, ask the lawyer to repeat it. He will probably ask the court reporter to read the question to you from his shorthand notes. If, after hearing it again, you still do not understand it, say so. If counsel persists in requiring an answer, you can always

161

turn to the judge for protection. He will make sure you are asked an understandable question.

3. *Don't venture a guess in answering a question.* If you do not know the answer to a question, say so. Never guess. Inferences are for the court or jury to make.

4. *Think before answering.* Give each question as much thought as is required for a responsible answer.

When opposing counsel asks you a question that is objected to by the attorney who called you as a witness, do not answer the question until the judge makes a ruling upon the objection. If any objection is raised during your answer, stop talking and wait for a ruling from the judge.

In announcing his ruling the judge may say "objection sustained," which means that the objection was a valid one and the question should not be answered by the witness. If the judge says "objection overruled," it means that the objection was without merit and that the question must be answered.

5. *Answer questions precisely and objectively.* In your answer, come directly to the point of the question. State the facts as you know them. Do not offer an opinion (e.g., the speed of a car) unless one is asked of you.

Do not volunteer information. Remember that you are a witness, not the prosecutor or defense counsel. Leave the presentation of evidence up to them. Your job is solely to testify to the facts, not to secure a conviction or an acquittal.

6. *Speak so that you can be heard.* In a jury case you must speak loudly enough for the jury to hear you. One reason many lawyers stand at the far end of the jury box when they ask their questions is that if they can hear your answers so can the jurors.

A witness should not put his hands to his mouth while he talks, nor should he ever chew gum.

Do not nod or shake your head in answer to a question. Some jurors, and even the judge, may not observe the head shake. Moreover, the court reporter who is recording your testimony in shorthand or on a stenotype machine will not be able to record your answer, and it will cause an interruption and a request for an audible answer.

7. *Be forthright with your answers.* When opposing counsel asks you a question, do not look to the lawyer who called you as a witness before giving your answer. Such a gesture may create the impression that you are reluctant to tell the truth and want some help to suppress it. If the question is understandable to you, be forthright with your answer. If, for any reason, the question is an improper one, counsel or the judge will exercise the responsibility of sparing you the answer.

8. *Testify in as positive a manner as circumstances permit.* Answer understandable questions without hedging. If you know you will be asked certain questions about the speed of a vehicle or the time of an occurrence, have the specific answers clearly in mind and state them in a positive manner, even though you may say "about 50 miles an hour" or "about ten o'clock."

9. *Maintain a correct posture.* A witness should sit up straight in the witness chair. He should avoid slouching, squirming, or turning around unnecessarily. Any such activity may become a distraction that will lessen the effectiveness of the testimony.

10. *Be courteous.* When addressing the judge, refer to him as "Your Honor." When opposing counsel asks you a question like "Are you sure?" respond with "Yes sir, I am" or "No, sir"—each is an effective courteous response.

11. *Be serious.* A courtroom is no place for wisecracks. Your testimony affects both the liberty (and possibly the life) of an individual and the protection of society. A per-

164   *The Citizen's Duty and Protection*

son who acts in a flippant manner may be regarded as a "smart aleck" by the jury and his testimony may be given little credence.

12. *Don't argue with counsel.* Never argue or fence with opposing counsel. You will rarely win because he is far better prepared to handle an encounter than you are. Even if you should win an argument, the jury may rate you a "wise guy" and may make an appropriate discount of your testimony.

13. *Do not lose your temper.* No matter how hard you are pressed, try not to lose your temper while under cross-examination. To do so will lessen your effectiveness as a witness. Some cross-examiners will make a deliberate effort to rattle you for the purpose of accomplishing that objective. If you succumb, you will be playing right into the hands of opposing counsel.

14. *Dress neatly.* First impressions are often received from the manner in which a person dresses. A jury's evaluation of a witness's testimony may be based on their first impression of him.

You should appear neatly dressed, but no witness should ever be flashy or overdressed. For example, a loud sport jacket, or a cocktail dress or micro-mini skirt or exotic hairdo, would not be appropriate. A business suit, white shirt, and tie for a male, and a modestly designed dress or suit for a female, are more suitable for the occasion.

In addition to the negative over-all impression that inappropriate attire can create, it can also distract and lessen the effectiveness of a witness's testimony.

15. *Be prepared.* Prior to appearing in court, the testimony of a witness should be discussed between the witness and the lawyer who has called him to testify. This is a perfectly ethical practice, and it is indispensable for effective testimony.

If you are asked on the witness stand whether you talked

to anyone about the case, respond unhesitatingly with "Yes." When asked with whom, say "With Attorney ———." Also admit, if asked, that you talked to other persons about the case, in the event that you did have other discussions.

16. *Avoid contacts with jurors.* Do not talk to, or in any way contact, any member of the jury sitting in the case in which you are appearing as a witness. Regardless of how innocuous or unrelated the matter you discussed may be to the case itself, such conduct may cause a mistrial or a reversal of the case on appeal, and you yourself may sustain considerable embarrassment.

Chapter 22

The Citizen's Legal Action Against Police

As discussed earlier, police misconduct in wrongfully seizing evidence may result in the acquittal of the suspect. In addition, the citizen is afforded other protections under the law against improper or corrupt police conduct. The police officer himself may be subject to criminal prosecution for improper official actions, and the citizen who is harmed by police misconduct may file a civil suit and recover monetary damages.

STATE CRIMINAL LIABILITY OF POLICE

The elements of many criminal offenses are such that an erring police officer might well fall within their scope. The following are some of the criminal offenses for which a police officer can be prosecuted for acts committed while serving in his official capacity.

Intimidation

A police officer who threatens to detain and question a relative of an accused person in order to induce the accused to cooperate is guilty of intimidation.

Extortion

A police officer who threatens a person with arrest or with physical brutality in order to procure money from that person is guilty of extortion.

Example

A police officer threatens a prostitute with arrest or physical violence unless she pays him a certain amount of money each week. The officer has committed the offense of extortion.

Coercing a Confession

Some states have laws which make it a crime to obtain a confession by means of physical force or by threat of physical force.

Example

A police officer, in attempting to obtain a confession, tells the accused that unless he cooperates some other police officers who are not as sympathetic as he might physically abuse him. The crime of coercion has been committed.

Assault and Battery

A police officer who threatens to abuse an accused person may be guilty of the crime of assault. If his threat is carried out, the offense of battery occurs.

Electronic Surveillance

Some states have laws against electronic surveillance (electronic eavesdropping and wiretapping). However, in most states electronic eavesdropping (as opposed to the tapping of a telephone line) is permissible when one party to the conversation has given consent to the eavesdropping. In such situations, a recording by the police officer is permissible.

Unauthorized Deadly Weapons

Although most police officers are permitted to carry concealed pistols, knives, and other weapons that an ordinary citizen is not permitted to carry, there are certain weapons that even a police officer, in most jurisdictions, is not permitted to carry. Usually listed among these prohibited weapons are gun silencers, sandclubs, brass knuckles, switchblade knives, and sawed-off shotguns.

Aiding Escape

It is a crime to help any prisoner escape from custody. A police officer who does not try to apprehend an escaping prisoner is guilty of this offense.

Perjury and Subornation of Perjury

A police officer-witness who knowingly testifies falsely in a criminal trial commits perjury. If an officer induces a witness to testify falsely, the officer is guilty of the crime of subornation of perjury. The false statement must be made under oath and it must be material to the issue before the court in order for a crime to be committed. The police officer must also know that the false statement is not true.

Harassing Witnesses or Jurors

It is a crime to harass or coerce a juror or witness regarding his participation in a criminal trial. A police officer who attempts to coerce a witness not to testify is guilty of this offense. A policeman who attempts to influence a juror, other than while testifying as a witness, also falls within this provision.

Bribery

It is a crime to offer or to accept a bribe. A bribe is something of value offered or accepted with the intention of influencing official performance. For example, a police officer who accepts a "gratuity" from a motorist in order to give the motorist a "pass" is guilty of bribery. Similarly, a police officer who offers a bribe to another public official is guilty of the offense. It is also a crime for a police officer to solicit a bribe from a citizen.

Failure to Report a Bribe

The statutes of many jurisdictions require a public official to report an attempted bribe to the prosecutor or to the chief of police. Failure to do so constitutes an offense. A police officer who fails to report an attempted bribe to his appropriate supervisor is guilty of this offense.

Tampering with Public Records

It is an offense to destroy, tamper with, or remove a public record. Therefore, a police officer who wrongfully alters a station's booking record or removes an arrest record violates this provision.

Official Misconduct

By state statute, it is a crime for a public official to exert his official authority to the detriment of another person in an unlawful manner. For example, a policeman who uses his office in order to collect money for a private collection firm is guilty of official misconduct.

Violating Rights of Accused

Many states have recently adopted legislation providing criminal penalties for police officers who violate specified statutory rights afforded to a person accused of a crime. For example, a police officer who refuses to permit an accused person to call his attorney may fall within this provision.

Although the instances of prosecution of police officers under state criminal statutes are infrequent, there is no question about their applicability to errant police conduct. In most states, the commission of any of these offenses, whether prosecuted or not, constitutes grounds for discharge of the officer from the force.

STATE CIVIL LIABILITY OF POLICE

Three types of civil tort cases for damage awards are frequently filed against police officers in connection with the performance of their duties. These are actions for false arrest and false imprisonment, malicious prosecution, and negligence.

False Arrest and Imprisonment

Since arrest and custody usually occur simultaneously, actions for false arrest often contain an additional count for false imprisonment, which is the unlawful restraint of an individual's personal liberty or freedom.

In addition to being a part of false arrest, false imprisonment may exist independently of false arrest. It might occur in a situation in which there is probable cause to make an arrest but later investigation indicates that the arrested person did not commit the crime and should be released. The police officer who persists in detaining the arrested person under such circumstances may be liable for false imprisonment, but only in those states that permit an officer to release an arrestee without a court order to that effect.

Malicious Prosecution

Malicious prosecution occurs whenever a police officer (or any other citizen) knowingly signs a complaint or causes a complaint to be signed against a person who he knows did not commit a crime. Malice is an essential element of malicious prosecution. The prosecution of a person with any motive other than that of bringing a guilty party to justice is a malicious prosecution, but this civil error is not established merely by the fact that the party bringing the suit was acquitted of a criminal charge.

Action for Negligence

A police officer who injures someone through ordinary negligence during the course of his official duties could be sued successfully in a civil proceeding. For example, a police officer who attempts to apprehend a suspect and fires his weapon negligently, thereby injuring an innocent bystander, is subject to civil liability. Negligent conduct in the use of a police vehicle also subjects an officer to civil liability.

Indemnification of Police Officers

A police officer is primarily liable for any judgment obtained against him, which means that he must pay out of his own pocket any money awarded to the person who successfully sues him. Most police officers do not have substantial finances, and ordinarily a large money judgment against one of them would be difficult to satisfy. To protect their officers, some jurisdictions have enacted indemnification statutes or ordinances which provide that the state, city, or county, as the case may be, will reimburse a police officer for any money damages awarded against him arising out of negligent conduct performed in the course of his official duties. Therefore, although a police officer may be without assets, the citizen, ultimately, will be compensated by the government employing the officer.

FEDERAL CRIMINAL LIABILITY OF POLICE

The Federal Civil Rights Act provides for criminal prosecution of police officers who deprive citizens of any federal right under the United States Constitution or the federal law. Federal prosecution is a consequence of the remedy of civil suit that is available to the victim of police misconduct under the Federal Civil Rights Act.

The most frequently invoked provisions of the Federal Civil Rights Act is that portion which reads as follows:

> Whoever, under color of any law, statute, ordinance, regulation or custom, willfully subjects any inhabitant of any State, Territory, or District to the deprivation of any rights, privileges, or immunities secured or protected by the Constitution or laws of the United States, or to different punishments, pains, or penalties, on account of such inhabitant being an alien, or by reason of his color, or race, than are prescribed for the punishment of citizens, shall be fined not more than $1,000 or imprisoned not more than one year, or both.

Examples
1. A police officer who tries to beat a confession out of a suspect.
2. A police officer who unlawfully searches an apartment without a warrant and without grounds for a search incident to an arrest.
3. A police officer who prohibits an individual from passing out religious pamphlets in a reasonable manner.
4. A police officer who, in making an arrest, uses excessive force because the arrested individual is a member of a minority group disliked by the police officer.

Criminal prosecution, like civil liability, under the Federal Civil Rights Act is limited to state, county, municipal, and other law enforcement officers. Federal law enforcement officers are excluded from criminal prosecution under the Act, with one exception: District of Columbia police officers, although not civilly liable under the Act, are subject to criminal prosecution.

Another Federal Civil Rights Act criminal provision that is often invoked reads as follows:

> If two or more persons conspire either to commit any offense against the United States, or to defraud the United States, or any agency thereof in any manner or for any purpose, and one or more of such persons do any act to effect the object of the conspiracy, each shall be fined not more than $10,000 or imprisoned not more than five years, or both.
>
> If, however, the offense, the commission of which is the object of the conspiracy, is a misdemeanor only, the punishment for such conspiracy shall not exceed the maximum punishment provided for such misdemeanor.

Still another section of the Civil Rights Act provides for criminal prosecutions for conspiracy. Police officers, as well as private persons who conspire with them, are subject to prosecution under this provision.

Example

A citizen loaned money at a high rate of interest and received a note as evidence of the loan. When the note was not paid on time, the citizen hired a police officer to collect the amount owed. The police officer, in uniform, visited the borrower, threatened arrest and beat the borrower in order to collect the money owed to the citizen. Both the citizen and the police officer are subject to prosecution under the Civil Rights Act.

Federal Civil Liability of Police

Since the landmark decision of the United States Supreme Court in 1961 *(Monroe v. Pape)*, the Federal Civil Rights Act has been used with increased frequency by private citizens seeking to recover damages against police officers for alleged wrongs received during the course of police performance. The provision of the Federal Civil Rights Act that is most frequently invoked in these cases reads as follows:

> Every person who, under color of any statute, ordinance, regulation, custom, or usage, of any State or Territory, subjects, or causes to be subjected, any citizen of the United States or other person within the jurisdiction thereof to the deprivation of any rights, privileges, or immunities secured by the Constitution and laws, shall be liable to the party injured in an action at law, suit in equity, or other proper proceedings for redress.

The Federal Civil Rights Act may be invoked against a state, county, municipal, or other local police official. It may not be invoked, however, against a federal law enforcement officer.

Example

A federal narcotics officer and a state police officer made a narcotics raid together. During the narcotics raid, they performed an unreasonable search and seizure and also beat the person in whose apartment the raid occurred. The state police officer can be sued, but the federal narcotics officer is immune from such suit, although he can be sued civilly in a state court.

In order for suit to occur under the Federal Civil Rights Act, the conduct that is the subject of the law suit must have been performed by a police officer "under color of" his official position. That means that if the police officer performs a wrong in the conduct of his duties as an officer, even though his conduct is beyond the scope of his proper duties or is prohibited by his department, he may be liable under the Federal Civil Rights Act. But when a police officer is clearly acting as a private citizen, he may not be sued under the Federal Civil Rights Act.

Example

On his night off, Officer Jones goes to a tavern, drinks too much, engages Citizen Al in a fight and breaks Al's jaw. The next day, while on duty and irritated by the effects of the previous night, Officer Jones uses excessive force in arresting Citizen Bob. Citizen Bob, who did not provoke Officer Jones in any manner, receives a broken jaw. Citizen Bob may invoke the Federal Civil Rights Act; Citizen Al may not. When Officer Jones struck Citizen Bob, he was acting in his official capacity; Citizen Al, however, was struck while Jones was acting as a private citizen. Citizen Al, of course, can still sue Officer Jones as a private citizen in a tort action.

Although the Federal Civil Rights Act may be invoked to collect damages for violation of "rights, privileges, or immunities secured by the [Federal] constitution and laws," it does not provide for redress for a violation by a police officer of a state constitution or a local law.

Example

Officer Brown arrests Citizen Kane. A state statute provides that upon making an arrest an officer must bring the arrested person before a magistrate within a two-hour period. Officer Brown delays three hours before bringing Kane before a magistrate. During that period, Kane is not interrogated by the police, nor is any other unlawful conduct performed. Kane may not sue Officer Brown under the Federal Civil Rights Act. Officer Brown deprived Kane of a right secured under a state statute, not under federal law or the United States Constitution.

The Federal Civil Rights Act provides for every type of relief available under the law, which means that the relief need not be limited to money damages.

Example

Fred Burns owns and operates a book store. The local ladies' club thinks that he sells dirty books. The police have examined the books that Burns sells and determined that they are not legally obscene. However, the president of the ladies' club is married to Officer White, who is assigned to the police district where Burns' book store is located. Every morning Officer White, influenced by his wife, goes to Burns' store, searches for dirty books, and seizes the books which his wife has told him about. Burns may file a Federal Civil Rights Act complaint against Officer White and, in addition to collecting money damages, may enjoin Officer White from coming into the book store and harassing him.

Wiretapping and Bugging

In 1968, Congress passed a law making it a criminal offense for anyone, without proper authorization, to use any electronic, mechanical, or other device to tap a telephone or intercept any other wire communication, or to intercept other oral communications that occur on the premises of, or that are related to the operation of, any commercial establishment engaged in interstate commerce.

The 1968 federal act also establishes the procedure whereby federal officers may be authorized to use electronic surveillance in the investigation of crime and criminals. This involves procurement of a court order specifically authorizing the particular surveillance desired by the investigators. Any federal officer who conducts an electronic surveillance other than through this means (unless he does so under a narrowly defined emergency stated in the statute) is guilty of a criminal offense. The same criminal liability attaches to any other person, including state and local law enforcement officers, who indulges in wiretapping or in the interception (by "bugging") of other oral communications affecting a business or any commercial establishment engaged in interstate commerce.

In order for non-federal law enforcement officers to wiretap or to conduct electronic surveillance, the states must enact statutes that conform strictly to the provisions of the federal enactment. In the absence of such legislation, there can be no wiretapping at all by state or local law enforcement officers, nor can they indulge in any other kind of electronic interception of oral communications affecting interstate business operations. The term "interstate business operations" has been liberally extended in other areas of federal law to include such facilities as a locally operated hotel.

Constitutional Provisions

The first eight Amendments are known as the Bill of Rights. They were originally intended, and at one time judicially interpreted, as restrictions on the federal government alone, not on the states. In recent years, the United States Supreme Court has held that a number of the provisions of the Bill of Rights—those that the Court considers essential to "fundamental fairness" in criminal trials—are applicable to the states by virtue of the guarantee in the Fourteenth Amendment that no *state* shall deprive any person of life, liberty, or property, without "due process of law."

The foregoing line of reasoning is illustrated in the so-called "exclusionary rule"—the court-developed rule that requires the rejection of evidence that has been obtained by an "unreasonable" police search or seizure. When originally created, the exclusionary rule was a rule of evidence, required only by federal courts in federal cases. It was not conceived as a constitutional requirement; the states, therefore, were at liberty to adopt or refuse to adopt the rule, and, shortly, they were about evenly divided over the issue. Later on, the Supreme Court elevated the exclusionary rule to a constitutional requirement, just as though it had been written into the Fourth Amendment after the prohibition against "unreasonable searches and seizures." In the 1961 case of *Mapp v. Ohio,* the Supreme Court held that the Fourth Amendment's protection and the exclusionary rule were elements of "due process" and, therefore, were binding upon all the states. As a consequence, no state court may now admit, in a criminal case, evidence secured as a result of an "unreasonable" search or seizure. Any "illegal" search or seizure is considered an "unreasonable one."

We quote here the provisions of the Constitution of the United States that are most frequently invoked by citizens for protection

179

against abuses of authority by the police. Comparable provisions are to be found in practically all state constitutions.

Preamble

We the People of the United States, in Order to form a more perfect Union, establish Justice, insure domestic Tranquility, provide for the common defense, promote the general Welfare, and secure the Blessings of Liberty to ourselves and our Posterity, do ordain and establish this Constitution for the United States of America.

Article I

Section 8.   The Congress shall have Power To lay and collect Taxes, Duties, Imposts and Excises, to pay the Debts and provide for the common Defense and general Welfare of the United States; but all Duties, Imposts and Excises shall be uniform throughout the United States . . .;

To regulate Commerce with foreign Nations, and among the several States and with the Indian Tribes . . .;

To provide for the Punishment of counterfeiting the Securities and current Coin of the United States . . .;

❊   ❊   ❊

To define and punish Piracies and Felonies committed on the high Seas, and Offences against the Law of Nations;

To declare War . . . and make Rules concerning Captures on Land and Water . . .;

To provide for calling forth the Militia to execute the Laws of the Union, suppress Insurrections and repel Invasions;

To provide for organizing, arming, and disciplining, the Militia, and for governing such Part of them as may be employed in the Service of the United States, reserving to the States respectively, the Appointment of the Officers, and the Authority of training the Militia according to the discipline prescribed by Congress;

To exercise exclusive Legislation in all Cases whatsoever, over such District (not exceeding ten Miles square) as may, by Cession of particular States, and the Acceptance of Congress, become the Seat of the Government of the United States, and to exercise like Authority over all Places purchased by the Consent of the Legislature of the State in which the Same shall be, for the Erection of Forts, Magazines, Arsenals, dock-Yards, and other needful Buildings;—And

To make all Laws which shall be necessary and proper for carrying into Execution the foregoing Powers, and all other Powers vested by this Constitution in the Government of the United States, or in any Department or Office thereof.

Section 9.   No . . . ex post facto Law shall be passed.

✣   ✣   ✣

Article III

Section 1.   The judicial Power of the United States, shall be vested in one supreme Court, and in such inferior Courts as the Congress may from time to time ordain and establish. The Judges, both of the supreme and inferior Courts, shall hold their Offices during good Behaviour, and shall, at stated Times, receive for their Services, a Compensation, which shall not be diminished during their Continuance in Office.

Section 2.   . . . the supreme Court shall have appellate Jurisdiction, both as to Law and Fact, with such Exceptions, and under such Regulations as the Congress shall make.

The Trial of all Crimes, except in Cases of Impeachment, shall be by Jury; and such Trial shall be held in the State where the said Crimes shall have been committed; but when not committed within any State, the Trial shall be at such Place or Places as the Congress may by Law have directed.

Section 3.   Treason against the United States, shall consist only in levying War against them, or in adhering to their Enemies, giving them Aid and Comfort. No person shall be convicted of Treason unless on the Testimony of two Witnesses to the same overt Act, or on Confession in open Court.

✣   ✣   ✣

Article VI

This Constitution, and the Laws of the United States which shall be made in Pursuance thereof; and all Treaties made, or which shall be made, under the Authority of the United States, shall be the supreme Law of the Land; and the Judges in every State shall be bound thereby, any Thing in the Constitution or Laws of any State to the Contrary notwithstanding.

AMENDMENTS

Amendment I

Congress shall make no law respecting an establishment of religion, or prohibiting the free exercise thereof; or abridging the freedom of speech, or of the press; or the right of the people peaceably to assemble, and to petition the Government for a redress of grievances.

182   *Appendix*

Amendment II
A well regulated militia, being necessary to the security of a free State, the right of the people to keep and bear arms, shall not be infringed.

Amendment III
No Soldier shall, in time of peace be quartered in any house, without the consent of the owner, nor in time of war, but in a manner to be prescribed by law.

Amendment IV
The right of the people to be secure in their persons, houses, papers, and effects, against unreasonable searches and seizures, shall not be violated, and no warrants shall issue, but upon probable cause, supported by oath or affirmation, and particularly describing the place to be searched, and the persons or things to be seized.

Amendment V
No person shall be held to answer for a capital, or otherwise infamous crime, unless on a presentment or indictment of a Grand Jury, except in cases arising in the land or naval forces, or in the militia, when in actual service in time of war or public danger; nor shall any person be subject for the same offence to be twice put in jeopardy of life or limb; nor shall be compelled in any criminal case to be a witness against himself, nor be deprived of life, liberty, or property, without due process of law; nor shall private property be taken for public use, without just compensation.

Amendment VI
In all criminal prosecutions, the accused shall enjoy the right to a speedy and public trial, by an impartial jury of the State and district wherein the crime shall have been committed, which district shall have been previously ascertained by law, and to be informed of the nature and cause of the accusation; to be confronted with the witnesses against him; to have compulsory process for obtaining witnesses in his favor, and to have the assistance of Counsel for his defence.

❋   ❋   ❋

Amendment VIII
Excessive bail shall not be required, nor excessive fines imposed, nor cruel and unusual punishments inflicted.

Amendment IX
The enumeration in the Constitution, of certain rights, shall not be construed to deny or disparage others retained by the people.

Amendment X

The powers not delegated to the United States by the Constitution, nor prohibited by it to the States, are reserved to the States respectively, or to the people.

✿   ✿   ✿

Amendment XIV

Section 1.   All persons born or naturalized in the United States, and subject to the jurisdiction thereof, are citizens of the United States and of the State wherein they reside. No State shall make or enforce any law which shall abridge the privileges or immunities of citizens of the United States; nor shall any State deprive any person of life, liberty, or property, without due process of law; nor deny to any person within its jurisdiction the equal protection of laws. . . .

Section 5.   The Congress shall have power to enforce, by appropriate legislation, the provisions of this article.

Glossary

Arraignment—a court proceeding at which the charge is read to the accused and the trial date is set. In the federal system, it also refers to the proceeding in which an arrestee is taken before a federal commissioner for the equivalent of a preliminary hearing within the state system.

Arrest Warrant—a document issued by a court authorizing the police to arrest a person for the commission of an offense.

Charge—an indictment or information.

Compounding a Crime—the crime of offering or receiving money for promising not to have a crime prosecuted.

Directed Verdict—an order by the judge (based upon an essential weakness of the prosecution's case) that the jury must find that the defendant was not proved guilty beyond a reasonable doubt.

Double Jeopardy—a constitutional concept which requires that an accused person not be tried twice for the same offense.

Extortion or *Intimidation*—the crime of compelling payment of money or specific conduct by an individual under threat of physical abuse or other harm.

Felony—a serious offense for which the penalty is usually either capital punishment or incarceration in a penitentiary for one year or more.

Grand Jury—a panel of citizens appointed by the court to determine whether or not there is probable cause (reasonable grounds) for a suspect to be tried for a felony.

Indictment or *True Bill*—a document voted and filed by a grand jury charging a person with, and requiring that he stand trial for, the commission of a felony.

184

Information—a document prepared by the prosecutor charging a person with, and requiring that he stand trial for, the commission of a misdemeanor.

Jury or *Petit Jury*—a panel of citizens selected by court process to determine whether the evidence offered at trial proves the accused guilty beyond a reasonable doubt.

Misdemeanor—an offense for which the penalty is usually either a fine or incarceration in a jail for less than a year.

Misprision of Felony—the crime of concealing one's knowledge of the commission of a felony.

Motion—a request, made either in writing or orally, that the court rule on a particular legal issue.

Nolo Contendere—a plea which has the same effect as a plea of guilty, except that it cannot be regarded as an admission of guilt in any civil trial.

Offense or *Crime*—a violation of a state statute for which a penalty is prescribed.

Penal Ordinance—legislation enacted by a political subdivision of a state (city or county) which sets forth a penalty for its violation.

Penal Statute—legislation enacted by a state legislature which sets forth a penalty for its violation.

Preliminary Hearing—a court proceeding to determine whether or not there is sufficient evidence against the accused to take the case to the grand jury or for him to stand trial. Known within the federal system as arraignment.

Quashing of Indictment—an order by the judge that the formal written document charging the accused with a felony is defective.

Search Warrant—a document issued by a court authorizing the police to search a place or a person (usually for evidence of an offense).

Subornation of Perjury—prevailing upon someone to lie under oath.

Suppression of Evidence—an order by the judge refusing to permit certain evidence to be considered against the defendant.

Tort—a civil wrong to a person that can be compensated by money damages but not by criminal penalty.

Venue—the place or court where a trial is to be held.

Index

Abortion, offense of, 39; death as result of, felony-murder, 39
Accessory, after the fact, 78; before the fact, 77; effect of change of mind, 78; in rape case, 15
Accomplice, penalty for being, 77
Addiction to Narcotics, addicts' unlawful acts, 51
Administrative Agencies, warrant requirements for searches, 141
Adultery, offense of, 17
Anonymous telephone calls, offense of, 20, 21
Appeals, effect of "reversed and remanded" decision, 104; from habeas corpus writ, 105; from quashing indictment, 95; nature and effect of, 104; suppression-of-evidence orders, 141; to federal courts, 104; to state appellate courts, 104
Arraignment, purpose and nature of, 94, 184
Arrest, alternatives to, 118; arrestee's right to early court presentation, 91; definition of, 109; false, civil suit for, 113, federal civil rights action for, 113; federal officer's right to, 118; force permissible in making, 121; "fresh pursuit," 120; hearsay evidence as basis for, 111; informers' tips as basis for, 111;

invalid, consequences of, 113; jurisdiction requirement, 120; limitations upon power to, 120–124; permissible search and seizure after, 129–131; post-arrest obligations, 121; without warrant, 109; with warrant, 113
Arson, offense of, 31
Assault, offense of, 13–15; penalties, 15
Attempt, offense of, 73; misapprehension of circumstances as defense, 74; "substantial" step requirement, 73
Battery, offense of, 13–15; penalties, 14
Bigamy, offense of, 17
Bribery, offense of, 60
Bugging; see Electronic Surveillance
Burglary, offense of, 27
Capital Punishment, felony-murder issue, 5; jury imposition of, 100; kidnapping penalty, 11; number of executions, 9
Certiorari, writ of, 105
Children, incapacity for criminal conduct, 84
Citizen Arrest, conditions required for, 123; force permissible in, 123; upon officer's request for assistance, 123
Citizen Remedies Against Police,

186

Homicide, definition of, 3; excusable, 3; federal law of, 8; justifiable, 3
Immunity, grant of, to compel testimony, 81, 82
Incest, offense of, 16
Indecent Liberties, offense of, 16
Indictment, motion to quash, 94; necessity in felony cases, 93
Information, charge filed by prosecutor, 93
Informers, tips of, 111
Insanity, at time of trial, 87; legal tests of, 86
Instructions to Jury, purpose of, 99
Interference with police, offense of, 65
Interrogations and Confessions, delay in arraignment, effect of, 145; evidence, admissibility of, 144; Miranda requirements, 146; promise of immunity or lenience, effect of, 142; required warnings of constitutional rights, 146; right to counsel, 146; trustworthiness as test of confession admissibility, 147; voluntariness as test of confession admissibility, 142, 147
Intoxication, defense of, 85; in public, offense of, 56
"Juice" loans, offense of, 62
Jury, communications with, prohibited, 69; direction by court to acquit, 98; "hung," 99; peremptory challenges in selection of, 97; right to trial by, 96; selection of, 97; selection of foreman for, 99
Kidnapping, offense of, 10; federal offense of, 11; penalty for, 10, 11
Larceny, definition of, 22; grand, 26; petit, 26
Larceny by Bailee, offense of, 24
Lindbergh Law, federal kidnapping offense, 11
Looting, offense of, 58
Malice, element of murder, 4, 5
Malicious Mischief, offense of, 32
Mann Act, federal offense, 19
Manslaughter, definition of, 5; involuntary, 5, 7; modern legislation, 9; voluntary, 5, 6
Marches, limitations upon and permits for, 59
Mayhem, offense of, 14

Mental Incompetence, as bar to prosecution, 87
Mental Responsibility, defenses, 84–85; "evil mind" requirement for, 83
Miranda Warnings, prerequisite to interrogation, 146; requirement "eliminated" by congress, 147
Misprision of Felony, offense of, 29, 30
Mob Action, offense of, 57; restitution from government for harm from, 57
Morals, offenses affecting the public, 33–65
Motions, change of venue, 95; pretrial, 94; quashing arrest warrants, 116; quashing indictment, 94; suppression of evidence, 95
Murder, definition of, 4; degrees of, 5; felony-murder, 4, 39; malice element, 4, 5; modern legislation, 9; second degree, 5
Narcotics, addiction to, 51; definition of, 47; federal laws against, 48, 49; glue sniffing, offense of, 50; hypodermic equipment prohibition, 49; possession by addicts, 51; prescription sales, 50; record keeping by lawful dispenser of, 49; state laws against, 48
Necessity, defense of, 85
Negligent Homicide, offense of, 7
Nolo Contendere Plea, effect of, 94
Notice to Appear, alternative to arrest, 118-119
Obscenity, offense of, 33; censorship of movies, legal requirements for, 37; child protection from, in movies, 37; difficulty of enforcing obscenity laws, 38; knowledge of nature of material, requirement of, 35, 36; legal procedures for declaring motion pictures obscene, 36, 37; license to show movies, effect of, 37; noncriminal, within home, 33; "scienter" requirement, 35–36; search warrant requirements, 38; supreme court's definition of, 38; technical prohibitions on law enforcement, 38; tests for determining, 33, 34; unprotected as free speech and free press, 33
Obstructing justice, devising means